FOR TED KESSLER

Contents

Preface

THE FOXTAIL GROUP OF WHITE PINES are exciting trees to discover, scattered like rare gems high in their mountain homes. The three species of this group—Great Basin bristlecone pine, Rocky Mountain bristlecone pine, and foxtail pine—survive where few other trees put down roots, and some of them seem to remain there forever. Their expressive shapes speak to the inner man and the inner woman as few trees do. Seen, smelled, or touched, they will lure you from one tree to the next, no matter how rocky the ground or how strong the wind. It is trite to say they inspire. But they inspire. As a lifelong lover of pine trees, I feel strongly that knowing something of the biology of these trees—their piney nature—will add pleasure for anyone walking among them and feeling their presence.

Great Basin bristlecone pine was christened "the world's oldest known living thing" by Edmund Schulman in a 1958 issue of *National Geographic Magazine*. Its longevity and striking appearance have made the species famous. Not all scientists agree with Schulman's claim, and pinning down the truth about it seems worth doing. Claims of great age also raise important biological and philosophical issues. For these reasons, this book looks closely at issues relating to longevity in trees.

Great Basin bristlecone pine has been enormously important to dendrochronology, the dating of the natural and human past by scientific analysis of tree rings. The techniques of tree-ring analysis, some of its major findings, and the training of its researchers owe much to Great Basin bristlecones of extended age, whose growth responds to subtle changes in climate. These trees are a scientific resource to be preserved, and the more we know about them the more we can learn in the future.

Curiosity about the foxtail and bristlecones, coupled with a lack of reader-friendly natural histories of these trees, has allowed a certain amount of misinformation and guesswork to cling to them. But despite the awe they inspire, foxtail pine and the bristlecones are, after all, pines, and they do what their DNA tells them to do—within the limits set by their environment—just like the other members of their tribe. I believe that demystifying these trees with facts will not detract from their appeal, but will enhance it, because fact trumps fancy. Of course, our knowledge of them is paltry compared with what we'd like to know, and we probably don't even know which questions would give us the most interesting answers. But we must start somewhere.

Acknowledgments

OVER MY YEARS OF INVOLVEMENT WITH THESE PINES, many colleagues have helped me with moral support, advice, penetrating questions, informative answers, transportation, directions, and what-have-you. They include the late William B. Critchfield of the Institute of Forest Genetics (USDA Forest Service), whose encyclopedic knowledge of pines was always made freely available to those who asked for it; and my former doctoral student at Utah State University, Kristina Connor, whose cheerful persistence helped uncover important information about the effects of aging. Thomas Harlan of the Laboratory of Tree-Ring Research of the University of Arizona was most generous in sharing his incomparable knowledge of the history of old-tree studies. Some others are Susan Colclazer (Bryce Canyon National Park); Tim Coonan and Dan Duriscoe (Death Valley National Park); Malinee Crapsey (Sequoia and Kings Canyon National Parks); Paul Henderson and Bruce Freet (Great Basin National Park); Steve Robinson (Cedar Breaks National Monument); John Louth, Dennis Orbus, Brian Miller, Lynna Walker, Ron Olofson, Patti

Wells, Joan Benner, and Carol Gerard (Inyo National Forest); John Shochat, Harvie Tibbs, and Paul Demeule (Humboldt National Forest); Paul Boos (Bureau of Land Management); Tom Ledig, Dave Johnson, Cindy Collins, and Det Vogler (Pacific Southwest Research Station, USDA Forest Service); Harold Fritts, William Robinson, the late Wes Ferguson, and the late Don Graybill (Laboratory of Tree-Ring Research, University of Arizona); Yan Linhart (University of Colorado); the late Donald R. Currey (University of Utah); Caleb "Tuck" Finch (University of Southern California); M. I. Bidartondo (University of California–Berkeley); Bob Blanchette (University of Minnesota); Michael P. Cohen, author of *A Garden of Bristlecones*; Diane Ryerson; Dana K. Bailey; Michael Frankis; LeRoy and Jean Johnson; Harry Hutchins; Jim Cornett; Frank Callahan; and Michael Rourke. Finally, thanks to my longtime trail companions—my wife Harriette and three generations of loyal spaniels.

CHAPTER 1
Three Cousins

THIS BOOK IS ABOUT THREE SPECIES of closely related American pine trees. One of them, Great Basin bristlecone pine (*Pinus longaeva*), has the starring role in this book because it is famous, more is known about it, and it attracts many more curious visitors. The other two, Rocky Mountain bristlecone pine (*Pinus aristata*) and foxtail pine (*Pinus balfouriana*), have supporting roles.

There are about 110 species of pine (members of the genus *Pinus*) in the world. About a third of these are called white pines, or soft pines. Usually the needles of soft pines are gathered into groups of five at the point where they attach to the branchlet (the main exceptions to this rule are pinyon pines). Three of these five-needled pines have been classified as Foxtail Pines (*Pinus*, subsection *Balfourianae*)—the three cousins of this book. They are the only members of this exclusive group, and they have a lot in common. All dwell in the high country of the western United States, living in rigorous climatic conditions. All are intolerant of shade and tend to grow in open woodlands or as isolated individuals. All begin life as orderly looking, symmetrical young trees, but evolve over the years into big, even massive, picturesque individuals. They add beauty, grace, mystery, and charm to their rugged surroundings.

The foxtail and bristlecones are extremely long-lived trees. Great Basin bristlecone pine has been known to live 4,862 years, which makes it the oldest known tree in the world. In this book you will meet a couple of the most ancient individuals. Rocky Mountain bristlecone pine and foxtail pine, while not in the same class as Great Basin bristlecone for longevity, are also considered to be long-lived species.

There are several reasons why they live so long. First of all, the trees themselves are well built for the long haul. Unlike most living things, they show no signs of senescence, or degeneration over time. These trees do not die of old age; they die when something kills them. The roots, trunks, and branches are arranged in semi-independent sections that contain damage when it occurs so that the whole tree is not harmed. Unlike those of other pines, the needle bundles of the foxtail and bristlecones can all give rise to new buds, allowing new branches to continually replace those that die.

The habitat of the three Foxtail Pine species also affects their great longevity. Because these trees live in a tough environment—cold, dry, and windy at high elevations—they escape many of their predators, which are eliminated or reduced in the harsher climate. Because there is very little undergrowth, fire is not carried into the rocky places where the trees grow. And fungi that rot wood are very slow growing in the dry climate. For these reasons, global warming could be very dangerous for the trees. As the

Geographic Distribution of the Bristlecone Pines and Foxtail Pine

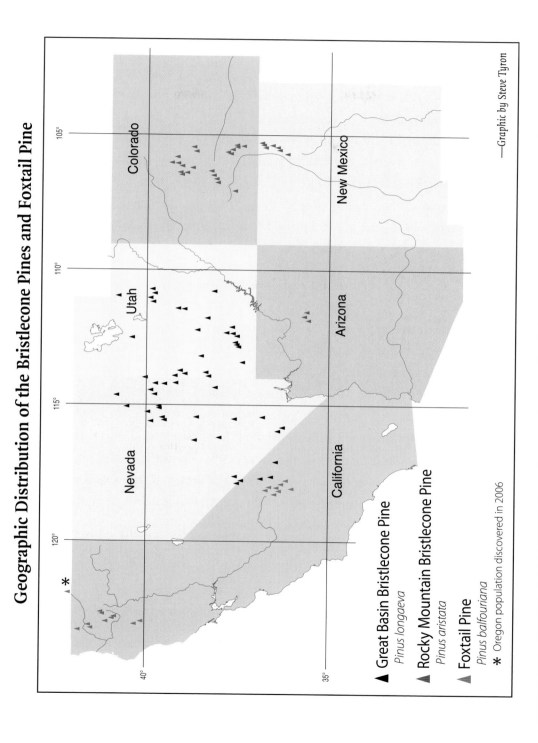

▲ Great Basin Bristlecone Pine
Pinus longaeva

▲ Rocky Mountain Bristlecone Pine
Pinus aristata

▲ Foxtail Pine
Pinus balfouriana

* Oregon population discovered in 2006

—Graphic by Steve Tyron

climate warms, populations gradually die back at the lower edges and retreat up into higher, cooler elevations, but they are already high on the mountains they inhabit and have almost nowhere else to go.

Although the three species of the Foxtail Pine group share significant characteristics, they are different enough to maintain separate identities. The foxtail pine was the first of the three species to be discovered, and thus it provides the group name. In this book, the group name Foxtail Pine is capitalized, and the name of the species foxtail pine is not.

Great Basin Bristlecone Pine
Pinus longaeva D. K. Bailey

The Great Basin bristlecone pine is the tree associated in the public mind with great longevity and picturesque form. Its scientific name has only been in use since the 1970s, as the trees were considered identical to Rocky Mountain bristlecone pines until Dana K. Bailey gave persuasive reasons to place them in a new species in 1970. The scientific name he proposed, *Pinus longaeva*, signifies that this is a long-lived member of the genus *Pinus*. Scientific names are in Latin and must conform to various legalisms to be accepted by botanists. But common names, like Great Basin bristlecone pine, have no such requirements and can respond to the marketplace of ideas. In this marketplace popularity determines legitimacy. Most people prefer the common name Great Basin bristlecone pine to intermountain or western bristlecone, both of which occasionally are used, but none of these names is more correct than the others.

An ancient Great Basin bristlecone pine, White Mountains, California. —*Photo by David Lanner*

Identification

A key fact in identifying any of the three Foxtail Pine species is that no two of them are ever found together in nature. So it is never necessary to separate them from each other, only from other five-needled pines with which they occur.

The only other five-needled pines found where Great Basin bristlecone grows are limber pine (*Pinus flexilis*), very frequently, and whitebark pine (*Pinus albicaulis*), very rarely. Curiously, all three of these five-needled pines grow together in just one known

FOLIAGE AND CONES OF THE GREAT
BASIN BRISTLECONE PINE. —*Photo by the author*

place: Thomas Canyon in Nevada's Ruby Mountains. Of these three pines, only Great Basin bristlecone has a fine, sharp bristle on each cone scale (pick up one and squeeze it), and short (0.75 to 1.5 inch), deep green needles densely massed on the last foot or two of the branchlets, giving the impression of tassels or bottlebrushes. The bark of young trees is smooth and gray, changing with age to furrowed and dark brown, and in old age becoming scaly and reddish brown.

Range

Stands of Great Basin bristlecone pine are found in eastern California in the White, Inyo, and Panamint Mountains. In Nevada they can be found on many high mountains, including the Quinn Canyon, Fish Creek, White Pine, Schell Creek, and Snake Ranges, and in the Ruby and Spring (Charleston) Mountains. Major Utah locations are the Deep Creek and Indian Peak Ranges; the Pine Valley, Wah Wah, and San Francisco Mountains; and the Markagunt and Aquarius Plateaus. This list is not exhaustive. Most stands are found between 9,000 and 11,500 feet.

Where to See Great Basin Bristlecone Pine

In California, Great Basin bristlecone pine is most conveniently seen in the Schulman and Patriarch Groves in the White Mountains, in an area dedicated to their preservation as the Ancient Bristlecone Pine Forest, within the Inyo National Forest. These groves can be reached by driving 13 miles east of Big Pine on California 168, then north on the narrow, winding, paved White Mountain Road for 7 miles. The visitor center at the Schulman Grove (at 10,100 feet) is an outstanding educational resource devoted almost entirely to the bristlecone pine. The Patriarch Grove (at 11,200 feet) is an additional 13 miles north.

In Nevada, the most accessible grove is in Great Basin National Park at 10,500 feet, 1.5 miles up the trail to Wheeler Peak. Las Vegas residents and visitors can see impressive Great Basin bristlecones in the Spring (Charleston) Mountains by hiking up the Lee Canyon Trail.

In southwestern Utah, Great Basin bristlecone pine is most easily visited along the Bristlecone Loop Trail at about 9,000 feet in Bryce Canyon National Park, and along short trails in Cedar Breaks National Monument.

Rocky Mountain Bristlecone Pine
Pinus aristata Engelmann

Rocky Mountain bristlecone pine was simply called bristlecone pine until it became necessary to distinguish it from the newly recognized Great Basin bristlecone. It is sometimes called eastern bristlecone, and in the dim past was called hickory pine. The species name *aristata*, meaning "bearded," refers to the bristles on the cone scales. The name was conferred in 1862 by Dr. George Engelmann, a mad-about-conifers St. Louis physician who was influential in making western American conifers known to science while anxious patients languished in his waiting room.

Identification

The only other five-needled pines found within the home range of Rocky Mountain bristlecone are limber pine and limber's close southern relative, southwestern white pine (*Pinus strobiformis*). Unlike these two pines, Rocky Mountain bristlecone has a fine,

TRAIL ETIQUETTE

Trail etiquette takes on a special importance when entering a grove of bristlecones or foxtails. Here you should regard every tree, even every stick on the ground, as being of enormous potential scientific value, and your goal should be to help preserve these trees and their surroundings. In the national parks and in the Ancient Bristlecone Pine Forest, rules are posted at visitor centers and on bulletin boards. These rules should be scrupulously observed. But even the less-famous populations of these trees may assume great importance in future research, so follow these practices in all groves of bristlecone and foxtail pines:

- Remove no specimens of branches, roots, or bark. Permits can be obtained for scientific collecting, but casual collecting is strongly discouraged. Violation of this basic rule has led to Methuselah—a Great Basin bristlecone almost five thousand years old—being vandalized and subsequently having its location kept from the public.

- Do not take dead wood for use as firewood or souvenirs. Dead wood can be dated by dendrochronology, and many specimens have proven vital in the past. For example, the use of dead wood has allowed dendrochronologists to capture climatic data extending about five thousand years further in the past than data from living trees.

- Walk on trails wherever provided. Make no erosive shortcuts between hairpin turns or switchbacks. Don't accelerate erosion by loosening rocks on steep slopes.

- Be satisfied with memorializing your visit to these remarkable trees by etching everlasting sights and smells on your brain, taking notes or photographs, making sketches—or buying this book.

sharp bristle on each cone scale, tassels at the ends of its branches, and conspicuous flecks of dried white resin on its needle surfaces. (Such flecks are occasional on Great Basin bristlecone as well, but are most characteristic of this species.) The needles are dark, glossy green, and 1 to 1.5 inches long. Bark color varies from smooth and gray on young trees to furrowed and reddish brown or grayish brown on older trees.

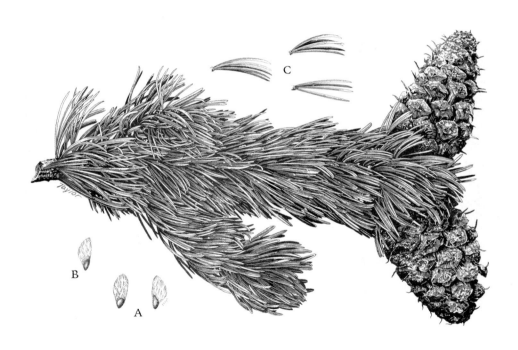

MATURE SEED CONES, NEEDLES, NEEDLE FASCICLES (C),
AND SEEDS (A, B) OF ROCKY MOUNTAIN BRISTLECONE PINE.
—*Taylor and A. E. Hoyle, plate 15 in Sudworth (1917)*

Range

Rocky Mountain bristlecone pine is found in central and south-central Colorado south of Rocky Mountain National Park, on Pikes Peak, the Spanish Peaks, and Mount Evans, and down the Sangre de Cristo Mountains into northern New Mexico. There is an outlying population in the San Francisco Peaks of northern Arizona. This list is not exhaustive. The elevation

ROCKY MOUNTAIN BRISTLECONE PINE, WINDY RIDGE, COLORADO. —*Photo by Brent Doerzman*

range of Rocky Mountain bristlecone pine is from about 7,500 to 11,700 feet.

Where to See Rocky Mountain Bristlecone Pine

In Colorado, Rocky Mountain bristlecone pine grows along the highway up Mount Evans. It can be seen from the highway in Cochetopa Pass between Saguache and Lake City, and at the end of an access road to Windy Ridge about 12 miles northwest of Fairplay, at an elevation of 11,714 feet.

In Arizona, an energetic hiker can see stunted bristlecones in the San Francisco Peaks along Humphreys Peak Trail at about 11,400 feet.

In northern New Mexico, bristlecones are found in the pristine Valle Vidal in the Sangre de Cristo Mountains, along Forest Road 1950, 27 miles southeast of Costilla. This is the largest stand of Rocky Mountain bristlecone pine, extending up the slope of 12,544-foot Little Costilla Peak.

Foxtail Pine
Pinus balfouriana Greville & Balfour

Foxtail pine was the first of the three Foxtail cousins to be discovered and described, and that priority is the reason the subsection that contains them was named *Balfourianae*. The common name "foxtail" refers to the "bottle-brush tassels" (John Muir's term) at the ends of the branches, caused by the densely set short needles that are retained for many years and therefore clothe the branch tips for up to a foot or more of their length. The scientific name honors Professor John Balfour, who helped bankroll the explorations of the tree's discoverer, John Jeffrey, back in 1852. The Sierra Nevada foxtail pine has been formally named subspecies *austrina*, indicating its southern location. The formal name for the Klamath Mountains foxtail pine is subspecies *balfouriana*, signifying that this is the subspecies originally given the species name, *balfouriana*.

Identification

Wherever foxtail pine grows, it is the only five-needled pine that has short (0.75 to 1.5 inch), stiff needles densely packed on tassel-like branchlets, with sharp tips painful to the touch. The Sierra

OPEN CONE, MATURING CONES, AND FOLIAGE OF SIERRA NEVADA FOXTAIL PINE. —*Photo by the author*

Nevada foxtail has bright red-orange bark on mature trunks and yellowish green foliage. The Klamath Mountains foxtail has gray bark and bluish green foliage.

Range

Californians had always pointed proudly to foxtail pine as a California endemic—a species growing naturally nowhere else Then, in 2006, professional tree seed collector Frank Callahan discovered a stand of foxtails in Oregon on Lake Peak, a 6,648-foot summit one mile north of the Oregon-California state line in the Rogue River and Siskiyou National Forests. This is now the northernmost outlier of a species whose major populations are found in two areas three hundred miles apart.

In northern California, where foxtail pine was first discovered, it grows in the ranges of the Klamath Mountains—the Scott, Marble, Salmon, Trinity, and Yolla Bolly Mountains, and the Trinity Alps. In the south, it grows in the Sierra Nevada, in Kings Canyon and Sequoia National Parks and on adjacent national forest lands. This list is not exhaustive. Its altitudinal range is from about 9,000 to 11,300 feet in the south, and 6,000 to 9,000 feet in the north.

Where to See Foxtail Pine

The Klamath Mountains population of foxtail pine is found at Lake Mountain Lookout (6,900 feet), ten miles east of Happy Camp via California 96 and Walker Creek Road. Hikers can see foxtail pine high on Mount Eddy via the Deadfall Creek Trail southwest of Weed. The Sierra Nevada population can be observed in Sequoia National Park, along a trail to Timber Gap and other hiking trails

14

SIERRA NEVADA FOXTAIL PINE AT TIMBER GAP,
SEQUOIA NATIONAL PARK, CALIFORNIA. —*Photo by David Lanner*

near Mineral King, and farther north on Alta Peak. From east of the park, foxtail pine can be seen in Kearsarge Pass, up the trail from the Onion Valley picnic area west of Independence.

Origins

The oldest fossils of a Foxtail-like species are from 46-million-year-old deposits from Thunder Mountain, Idaho. They have been classified as the fossil species *Pinus balfouroides* because they look like the present-day foxtail pine. Another fossil species, *Pinus crossii*, which looks much like Rocky Mountain bristlecone, has been found in Nevada (42 million years old), New Mexico (32 million), and Colorado (27 million). So it appears that species of the Foxtail Pine group have been living in these western mountains for more than 40 million years. When we view them today, we are gazing upon an ancient and durable tribe of conifers.

Botanists have addressed the question of "which begat which." All begin with a hypothetical common ancestor but then diverge in reconstructing a line of descent leading to the species of today's Foxtail Pine group. Such reconstructions are highly speculative, and beyond the scope of this book, so we will fast-forward to the ice ages of the Pleistocene (the past million years or so) to pick up the trail of these pines.

All three Foxtail species probably expanded their ranges downslope during the cool glacial periods of the ice ages, and retreated upslope during the interglacial periods. Remains of a foxtail pine cone found near Clear Lake, California, about 5,000 feet lower than today's northern population of foxtail pines, illustrates the magnitude of an ice age expansion. There is evidence that between

CREATIONISTS DISCOVER BRISTLECONE PINE

Ancient bristlecone pines have been a problem for "young earth creationists," who take the biblical account of creation literally. They believe that Noah's flood occurred about 4,000 years ago and that it uprooted all existing trees or buried them in sediments. Therefore, new trees that grew up after the flood cannot have many more than about 4,000 annual rings. On the other hand, creationists know that several Great Basin bristlecones exceed 4,600 rings, and that Prometheus (also called "the Currey tree"), from Wheeler Peak, Nevada, had at least 4,862 annual rings when it was felled in 1964. They counter this unfriendly evidence by suggesting that extra annual rings were added in wet years, or that trees were created with their rings already in place.

The first suggestion, which relies on the formation of large numbers of "false rings," is contradicted by research showing such rings to be extremely uncommon in bristlecones growing in harsh sites. The second notion can be neither proved nor disproved, so it cannot be evaluated by the means of science.

25,000 and 11,000 years ago, Great Basin bristlecone formed extensive woodlands with limber pine and Engelmann spruce (*Picea engelmanii*) on the lower slopes and valley bottoms of the Great Basin from the Wasatch Mountains to the Sierra Nevada. With the passing of the ice ages, the warming trend forced all three species of the Foxtail Pine group to higher and higher elevations in their search for ecologically suitable habitats.

Today the foxtail and bristlecone pines reside on high mountains, with nowhere to go if the climate warms beyond their physiological tolerances. Their subalpine habitats impose tough growing conditions—low temperatures, short growing seasons, drying winds, and summer drought, on shallow, rocky soils low in nutrients. Yet they persevere for extraordinarily long lives: Precise counts of annual rings on living trees have yielded up to 2,110 years for foxtail pine, and 2,435 for Rocky Mountain bristlecone. A Great Basin bristlecone had 4,862 rings when it was cut down. The nature of the durable and persistent trees that succeed under such conditions, and how they react to their environment, are explored in the next few chapters.

CHAPTER 2
What Pines Are Made Of

THE COMPLEX BEAUTY OF A TREE may seem beyond understanding, but trees build themselves in logical and consistent
ways, and we can analyze their structure using little more than
our eyes. So let us step into a bristlecone pine woodland and
visually take a pine tree apart. The information in this chapter
applies to pine trees in general unless specified otherwise.
Because more research has been done on Great Basin bristlecone pine than on the other two Foxtail Pines, data in this chapter
is sometimes available only for the Great Basin bristlecone.

Buds

Buds are the cylindrical, pointed, brown objects found at the tips
of shoots. Vigorous shoots high in the tree and in full sun have
a long leading bud pointing straight ahead, and they may have
some shorter side buds attached at the base of the leading bud.
From fall through spring they lie dormant, covered by overlapping
scales. They awake in late June or July, when the accumulated heat
of the season triggers their growth.

SHOOTS OF ROCKY MOUNTAIN BRISTLECONE PINE WHOSE
NEEDLES HAVE BEEN PLUCKED TO SHOW THE FASCICLES WITHIN
WHICH THEY ORIGINATED. —*Photo by the author*

The routine emergence of interfoliar buds from within the needle fascicles distinguishes the three Foxtail species from all other pines. Some other pines can also make branches that grow out from interfoliar buds, but only after injury. The three Foxtail cousins do it all the time. This trait may contribute to their survivability by allowing even old and battered trees to constantly regenerate their crowns, and it produces the dense masses of epicormic branches found on the trunks and limbs of middle-aged and old trees.

Needles

A pine needle is like a skyscraper. It has a stiff outer skin penetrated by rows of microscopic openings called stomates, which provide access to the outside air, like windows in a building. A needle has hundreds of flat plates of chlorophyll-bearing cells dividing its length into compartments, like the floors of a skyscraper. In a needle, liquid sap bathes the walls and floors of the compartments. The utility columns and elevator shafts that penetrate the floors of a skyscraper are analogous to the needle's resin canals and the vascular bundles that conduct liquids.

A vascular bundle is a prominent cylinder containing two pipes running down the center of the needle. One of the pipes is connected through the base of the needle to the wood of the branchlet. It conducts the soil water sucked up by the roots and pulled upward as a capillary column through the trunk and branches, to finally arrive in the needle. The other pipe of the vascular bundle carries the sugar solution formed in photosynthesis down through the needle and the inner bark of the branches, trunk, and roots. The

23

solution carried in the wood is the xylem sap, and the solution in the inner bark is the phloem sap. The water for both enters the roots from the soil.

The skin of a pine needle is made of epidermis cells overlaid by a waxy cuticle. The inner surfaces are streaked with white wax and contain the stomates. The stomates of all pine needles let carbon dioxide in and oxygen and water vapor out, facilitating photosynthesis. The needles of the Foxtail group and some other pines conserve water by forming loose plugs of wax in the stomates and by restricting stomates to the more protected inner surfaces. In foxtail and bristlecone pines, the outer needle surface is glossy green and lacks stomates. In addition, the tassel-like shoots of the three species of Foxtail Pine are flexible enough to "go with the flow" when a strong wind blows, exposing only the nonstomatal needle surfaces to the wind.

In addition to these water-saving features, the five needles of a fascicle pack closely together, especially those of Great Basin bristlecone pine. As do those of all five-needled pines, the needles of the Foxtail group fit together to form a cylinder, with each needle's cross section shaped like a slice of pie. During the heat of the day they close up, conserving the water inside the needle.

Immature needles do not make enough carbohydrates to grow on. They "appeal" for additional carbohydrates stored in older needles by sending growth hormones down the phloem into the older needles. Stored carbohydrates then move to the active new growth areas above. By the end of the summer, the newly matured needles are making more than enough carbohydrates to meet their needs, and they are storing the excess to help fill next year's

GREAT BASIN BRISTLECONE PINE, SHOWING ANNUAL GROWTH OF BRANCHES, WITH THE YEARS DELINEATED BY NEEDLES OF VARYING LENGTH. WHITE MOUNTAINS, CALIFORNIA. —*Photo by David Lanner*

needs. Thus each annual growth cycle is subsidized by savings from the previous year. During a Great Basin bristlecone pine needle's lifetime, it forms new phloem annually, it maintains its chlorophyll content, and its tough cuticle hardly degrades at all.

Needles of the foxtail and bristlecones have a maximum attainable length of about 1.5 inches. But spring drought, and possibly cool summer temperatures, can prevent needles from reaching that length, leading to annual variations of needle length along the shoot. Needles of the Great Basin bristlecone pine and the Klamath Mountains foxtail pine may live up to forty-five years.

Seed Cones

In July an alert observer will notice prickly 0.25-inch spheres at some of the shoot tips, especially high in the tree or on low limbs that sweep out into the sunlight. These are the new crop of immature seed cones, also called conelets. They will spread their scales so that grains of airborne pollen can enter the two tiny ovules on each scale's inner surface. For conifers, this is pollination. Then the ovules close up, the scales shut tight, and the young seed cone grows a bit before going dormant for the winter.

Next spring, the nucleus of a male sperm cell from a pollen grain trapped in each ovule will fuse with the nucleus of a female egg cell deep in the ovule. This is fertilization in conifers. The fertilized egg will develop into an embryo, and the tissue surrounding it will fuel its growth. (In a pine nut, like those harvested from pinyon pines, it is this nutritive material that we and wildlife eat.) The seed cone, purple and resinous, grows rapidly to full size. By late September to October it is light brown and about 3 inches long, with 0.25-inch bristles. It dries out, spreads its scales, and lets the seeds fall free. Aided by a long papery wing, the seed is carried in the wind. By next year most of the empty cones will have fallen off the tree. A new crop of cones will take form inside the buds of the more vigorous shoots.

A big crop of mature cones full of nutrient-packed seeds is a sizable investment for a pine tree, and most only produce big crops every few years. One would expect Great Basin bristlecone, which lives in such stressful environments, to produce a large crop of cones only rarely. But, paradoxically, it seems to produce cones in most years, much more frequently than its neighbors, limber pine and singleleaf pinyon (Pinus monophylla). The growth of its cones and seeds is fueled by stored carbohydrates, as well as by carbohydrates formed during the cones' growth surge. The growing cones themselves contribute a bit of carbohydrate too, from their own photosynthesis. In numerous conifers a big cone crop has been found to use food that would otherwise go into a larger growth ring in the trunk. Great Basin bristlecones have been reported not to sacrifice wood production to cones and seeds. This disparity needs to be verified by further investigation.

Pollen Cones

Pollen cones, sometimes incorrectly called catkins or male flowers, are the brightly colored 0.5-inch-long oval objects found in bunches just below the new needles on shoots in the lower crown. Their pollen sacs rupture in mid- to late July, releasing masses of dustlike pollen grains into the air. Tap a branch bearing mature pollen cones, and a yellow cloud will rise up through the canopy to disperse in the wind. If you are lucky, you may view a pollinating forest from a distance on a windy day and see billions of yellow grains surging like dust clouds. Pine pollen grains are tiny and buoyant enough to be carried many miles in the wind. That is why it is so surprising that foxtail pine pollen grains from the Sierra Nevada—which must surely cross the Owens Valley in large numbers on a prevailing westerly—seem not to have hybridized the Great Basin bristlecones of the White or Inyo Mountains despite the experimentally proven ability of the two species to cross.

RIPENING POLLEN CONES OF GREAT BASIN BRISTLECONE PINE IN THE WHITE MOUNTAINS, CALIFORNIA, IN EARLY JULY. —*Photo by the author*

After releasing their pollen, the pollen cones shrivel, fall from the tree, and become part of the forest floor litter. New pollen cones for next year will form inside the buds of weak shoots.

Seeds

Bristlecone and foxtail pine seeds consist of a nut about a quarter-inch to a third-inch long with an oval wing twice that length. They are tan to light brown with dark speckles. In the bristlecones, the wings cling to the nut with pincerlike forks and can be removed, but in foxtail pine the wings are rigidly attached to the nut. While in the cone, the seeds rest on the inner surface of a cone scale, wing pointing out. When a seed exits the cone, a mysterious, translucent light-brown "shadow" of its wing stays behind to ornament the place where it rested. A seed-bearing scale has the potential to bear two seeds, but lack of pollination, genetic incompatibility, feeding activities of insects, or other miniature calamities may prevent that potential from being met.

When they fall from the cone, seeds "helicopter" to the ground, languidly rotating in still air, beating against rocks and tree trunks in a stiff breeze, and possibly being dispersed over miles. Such dispersal ends when a seed comes to rest on the ground, becoming easy prey to foraging birds and small mammals and vulnerable to desiccation.

Some Great Basin bristlecone pine seeds are removed from their cones by Clark's nutcracker, a gray, black, and white relative of the jay that is common wherever foxtails or bristlecones grow. Nutcrackers have been seen harvesting seeds of Sierra Nevada foxtail pine from their cones. Unripe foxtail and Great Basin bristlecone pine cones have been found bearing the shredded scales inflicted by the hammering bills of foraging nutcrackers. Nutcrackers eat some seeds but store others under an inch or two of soil; the buried seeds, if not retrieved, can germinate and

THE COLORS OF CONES

Most Great Basin bristlecones have deep red pollen cones and dark purple seed cones. But a sizable minority have yellow pollen cones and green seed cones. This is easily observed in the summer, especially in July, when pollen is ready to be shed and the maturing seed cones that were pollinated a year ago are several inches long and conspicuous at the ends of branches.

Why the color variation? The trees with yellow/green cones lack the pigment anthocyanin, the same substance that makes apple skins red, maple leaves crimson, and grapes purple. The scant research that has been done on this color variation found a ratio of about four red/purple cones to one yellow/green in the White Mountains. This suggests there might be a dominant gene for anthocyanin in Great Basin bristlecone. If so, we would expect about 25 percent of the trees to lack the pigment and have yellow/green cones, or a ratio of three to one. Hikers on the Schulman Grove's Methuselah Walk in July should keep their eyes peeled to further test that ratio.

A very few Great Basin bristlecones have green seed cones that appear to be turning purple, and yellow pollen cones with reddish tips. And one 2,500- to 3,000-year-old Great Basin bristlecone in the Schulman Grove has been found to produce white pollen from its red pollen cones.

Rocky Mountain bristlecone and foxtail pines have yellow pollen cones and purple seed cones.

become seedlings. Survival rates of seeds dispersed by wind or by nutcrackers are unknown. It seems logical that seeds buried at "gardener's depth," invisible to rodents and protected from drying, should survive at a higher rate than those spread willy-nilly over the landscape by random gusts. That is the case with whitebark pine, but no data are available on any of the three Foxtail species.

Roots

Pines roots grow in the spring, when the snow has melted and the soil has warmed, and again in the fall if there is enough moisture in the soil. Pine root wood is less rigid and resinous than branch wood, and it has thinner bark. In rocky terrain, roots wrap tightly around boulders, forming a strong anchorage, and they seek water in cracks in the rocks. Like most pine roots, Great Basin bristlecone roots stay close to the surface, mainly in the first foot of soil, and there is usually no taproot. Instead, lateral mother roots leave the trunk like the arms of an octopus, sinuously passing to the side of the roots of neighbors and extending as far as 50 feet. They are often clearly visible on slopes where soil erosion has exposed them. (See photo on page 5.)

Pine mother roots subdivide into finer roots that bear new white tips during the spring growth flush. Most of those tender tips die within days or weeks. Luckier ones form a beneficial symbiosis with fungi living in the soil, in which the fungal tissue covers the root tips like a glove covering fingers. These roots will live several months and be replaced the next year. During that brief lifetime, the mycorrhizal tips will outperform non-mycorrhizal tips in the uptake of water and nutrients, and they may even ward off root-rotting fungi. Compared to the relatively fungus-rich soils of lower-elevation forests, the soils of Great Basin bristlecone stands in the White Mountains have been found to harbor only a few species of fungi capable of linking up with the pines' roots. The fine roots are of great importance in drawing up soil water with its hoard of dissolved minerals, but water is absorbed through the bark of larger roots as well.

Valmore C. LaMarche Jr., of the University of Arizona's Laboratory of Tree-Ring Research, showed in 1963 that the roots of very old Great Basin bristlecones often form buttresses, or walls of root wood, extending from the tree trunk along the ground. These buttresses are up to 3 feet in height (with about a foot of that beneath the soil) and about 6 inches thick. They form this way because, after growing for perhaps several hundred years, soil erosion begins to uncover them, killing the cambium on their upper surface and sides. But the cambium on the lower surface stays alive and adds new wood annually. Some of LaMarche's buttress roots had been growing only on their lower surface for 2,500 years, reducing their ability to deliver water to the parent tree. Buttresses resting on rocky soil and unable to penetrate deeper might exert an upward force that slowly raises the level of the tree.

Great Basin bristlecone is one of several tree species in which water moves from the major roots to sectors of the trunk directly above them, with little or no transfer around the circumference. More will be said of sectored architecture in Chapter 4.

Trees that grow in dry places may enhance their water-gathering ability in some creative ways. For example, it is very common for a tree's roots to form anatomically integrated grafts with the roots

32

of other trees of the same species. Water, hormones, and sugar solutions can pass through these grafts from tree to tree. If one such tree should die, its root system may be preempted by the trees to which it is grafted, thus making more water available to the survivors. Another way a tree can optimize its water resources is to draw excess soil water from wetter areas tapped by its root system, and to pump some of it out into drier areas in the soil, making it available for later uptake. This mechanism of hydraulic redistribution has been found in ponderosa pine (*Pinus ponderosa*) but not specifically in bristlecone or foxtail pines. Further research is awaited.

Wood

Wood is tissue that supports the tree physically, stores carbohydrates in specialized cells, and allows for the transport of water and dissolved minerals (sap). Wood is also called xylem, from the Greek word for wood, *xylon*. By extension, other tissues that move water are also classified as xylem even if they are not woody, like the vascular tissue in needles and young shoots.

The wood of pines is simpler than that of most trees. More than 90 percent of it is made up of narrow cells about one-sixth inch long, tapered at both ends and lined up with the long axis of the trunk, branch, or root. These cells, called tracheids, give conifer wood its strength and stiffness.

After a few weeks of life, the tracheids die, their contents disintegrate, and they become hollowed-out water pipes. The cell walls have openings, called pits, which allow tracheids to transport water from one to another, forming a continuous sap stream from roots to needles. The tracheids are collectively known as sapwood.

The sapwood of soft pines, including the foxtail and bristle-cones, is creamy in color. Eventually, deposits of mineral and organic matter clog the tracheids, and water can no longer move freely. The wood darkens, and in the Foxtail Pine group and many other pines it becomes reddish and strongly aromatic. It is then called heartwood. Since it takes years for heartwood to form, the tree always has outer rings of sapwood for water transport. The strength of heartwood is vital in keeping the tree erect, and it is more resistant to decay than sapwood.

Ray cells are the next most common component of pinewood, accounting for about 10 percent of its bulk. They appear on a stem cross section like fine radii extending to the inner bark from deep in the wood, but they are difficult to see in the foxtail and bristlecones unless observed with magnification on a smooth surface. Rays are one to several cells wide and tall, and sometimes contain a resin canal. In the view of structural engineer Claus Mattheck, rays pin the annual rings together so they do not slip against each other when the tree bends in the wind.

According to bristlecone researcher Kristina Connor, ray cells of Great Basin bristlecone can stay alive at least 140 years, which indicates a long life for sapwood in this species.

Cambium

Tracheids and ray cells are formed by the vascular cambium, a marvelous innovation in plant evolution. Most of us have looked at cambium without seeing it. Imagine driving into a campground in midsummer and striking the edge of a tree with your car's bumper; a piece of bark peels off, exposing a slick, moist patch of bare wood. The cambium is the slimy, paper-thin, transparent layer of tissue coating the bare surface. Though not much to look at, it accomplishes remarkable things: it builds giants. In a perfect, undamaged tree, a sheet of this tissue one to several cells thick would fit like a leotard between the wood and bark of every square inch of trunk, branch, and root.

The cambium sleeps through the winter. When spring warming stimulates bud growth, the developing foliage inside the bud dispatches a downward flow of growth hormones through the inner bark, which wakes up the cambium throughout the tree. The cells of the cambial sheet divide and the newly created cells enlarge, making the sheet thicker. New cells on the inner side of the sheet develop into tracheids and ray cells, which form the xylem, or wood. Cells formed on the outside of the cambial sheet develop into sieve tubes and ray cells, which form the phloem, or inner bark.

Sieve cells are tracheid-like cells that conduct phloem sap, hormones, and other substances from one part of the tree to another. A lot more wood cells will be formed annually than inner bark cells. The inner bark will be crushed each year by the advancing circle of cambium pushed forward by new wood, and the dead cells will be shed with other bark tissues. That's why there is so much more wood in a tree than there is inner bark.

Earlywood, Latewood, and the Annual Ring

Cambial cells are either long, narrow, and tapered at both ends, dividing to form tracheids; or they are quadrangular, dividing to form ray cells. These divisions of the cambial cells continue throughout the summer in the foxtail and bristlecone pines.

Tracheids formed early in the season become fat, but their walls remain thin. Those formed later remain thin, but their walls become thick and strong, reinforced with lignin, a natural polymer that strengthens cell walls. When seen in a piece of timber, the earlywood is light in color, and there is a gradual transition from the light color to the denser and darker latewood. The earlywood and latewood of a given year comprise that year's annual ring. At season's end, the cambium lies outside the edge of the new latewood and just inside the inner bark. The sharp line of demarcation between the last of the dark latewood and the beginning of the next year's light-colored earlywood allows us to count the annual rings and determine age.

The hormonal flow that triggers cambial growth occurs only once a year, because the initiation of bud growth and the elongation of new needles occur only once. That is why only one ring is formed each year. An exception to the correspondence of ring number and age occurs when part of the cambium fails to activate, thus forming no ring along part of the stem. This is common in heavily shaded trees, and even in Great Basin bristlecones in full sun and stressed by drought. The missing rings are usually present on other radii of the trunk or branch being sampled. The skimpy foliage of seedlings produces barely enough growth hormone to trigger cambial growth, and a clear-cut ring structure may be absent. This makes it difficult to accurately age seedlings, even with the aid of a microscope.

In the habitats of foxtail pine and the bristlecones, the annual ring is usually thin, and it can be extremely thin under drought or cold conditions. In Great Basin bristlecone it is not uncommon

CROSS SECTION OF AN OLD GREAT BASIN BRISTLECONE PINE
REMNANT FROM THE WHITE MOUNTAINS, CALIFORNIA.
DARK HORIZONTAL LINES ARE LATEWOOD WITH LIGHTER
EARLYWOOD BETWEEN. VERTICAL LINES ARE RAYS. DOTS
ARE LONGITUDINAL RESIN CANALS. —*Photo by Tom Harlan*

to find 100 to 200 rings per inch of radius. By contrast, a fast-growing coast redwood (*Sequoia sempevirens*) can form annual rings an inch thick. Slow growth produces wood with a higher proportion of latewood than does rapid growth, so the wood of Great Basin bristlecones is denser and stronger than that of most pines. The trunks of fallen Great Basin bristlecones lie in the sun, exposed to drying winds and cold blasts of air for thousands of years before they decay. Thin curls of wood, one to a few annual rings thick, peel off one by one in a slow process of reduction.

Spiral Grain

Tracheids do not always arrange themselves perfectly parallel to the stem's axis; they are often tilted, sometimes quite steeply. In different years a tree's grain may even spiral in different directions. When the bark is off a tree, you can see the spiraling grain that results from this variation. The cause of spiral grain has long been a subject of speculation, including theories about the direction of cambial cell divisions, influence of the earth's rotation, vague genetic characteristics, wind torque, growth rate, asymmetry in the root system, age, and species. It has been suggested by bio-mechanics scientist Roland Ennos that twisted fibers make a tree more flexible and thus less likely to break in the wind. Mechanical and mathematical analyses have computed stresses and optimized grain angles, but unfortunately none of this work has managed to explain just how a tree goes about laying down tilted tracheids.

Resin

Pines of all species produce great quantities of oleoresin, also called resin or pitch. Chemically, pine oleoresin has a solid rosin ingredient and a turpentine fraction that has been used for centuries as a commercial paint thinner and solvent. Turpentine contains mixtures of hydrocarbons known as terpenes, which are usually unique to a pine species. However, wood resin chemistry can vary within a species more than between species of the Foxtail Pine group. For example, wood resin of Rocky Mountain bristlecones in Arizona's San Francisco Peaks is more like the resin of Great Basin bristlecones in the Panamint Mountains above Death Valley than it is like that of Rocky Mountain bristlecones in Colorado and New Mexico.

Resin is viscous, sticky, and aromatic. It is made in resin ducts, or canals, that open up spontaneously in the tree's tissues. While new tracheids are being formed by the cambium, scattered gaps appear among them, forming open canals that run vertically within the new annual ring. The canals soon become lined with thin-walled cells that manufacture resin. Resin canals also form within wood rays, and these become longer each year as the ray is prolonged into new annual rings, and even into the new phloem.

Some anatomical studies show vertical and horizontal resin canals forming junctions, suggesting that the resin canals in a tree trunk are part of a coordinated system. If that is the case, such a massive network of resin-transmitting ducts could have important consequences for tree biology. For example, it raises the question of whether a tree can mobilize resin to counter bark beetle attacks occurring at some distance from the sources of the resin. Hydrostatic pressure in the resin canals forces resin out whenever a canal is cut. Bark beetles boring into a pine encounter the resin system as the tree's first line of defense. A tree supplied with lots of water and full canals can pitch out beetles more readily than a water-stressed tree, and many an ambitious bark beetle has been unceremoniously ejected with its boring dust, belly up, the victim of a pitch flow.

Resin canals are found in wood, inner bark, needles, cones, and sparingly in roots. Those in needles are completely contained within the needle. Even seed cones are plentifully supplied with resin canals, and they frequently drip gobs of sticky pitch. Almost any wound on a pine gets covered with resin, and the wound trauma triggers the formation of new resin canals in nearby tissue. Resin accumulations make pine heartwood an exceptional fuel with an incomparable palette of aromas. Resin must be handled to be appreciated; some favorite solvents for removing resin from sticky hands are cooking oil and lanolin.

Bark

Bark includes all the tissues outside the vascular cambium. It insulates the cambium from impacts and the heat of fires, prevents the cambium from drying out, and even helps to stiffen the stem. A first-year shoot is covered with a green or reddish-tinged epidermis. This is replaced the next year by a cortex that forms beneath the epidermis and gives the stem a smooth, grayish look. Eventually, a cork cambium forms in the cortex, which creates rough bark each year. Growth stresses fragment the cork cambium into a patchwork, and this leads to the furrowed, fissured, and flaky bark of pines. Bark also includes crushed phloem cells shed from the stem.

When bark is forcefully removed from pines—for example, by lightning, porcupine feeding, or impacts from falling rocks or trees—the cambium on the exposed surface dies and is never restored. The bare wood is usually covered by a copious flow of resin, which dries and forms a protective barrier against infection. The edges of wounds close up rapidly in fast-growing trees, but sometimes perhaps not at all in slow growers like the foxtail and bristlecones.

A mature Sierra Nevada foxtail pine with characteristic bark and epicormic branches, at Kearsarge Pass, California. —*Photo by the author*

Observations of Early Plant Explorers

On the Great Basin bristlecone pine

"About a foot or eighteen inches of the ends of the branches is densely packed with stiff outstanding needles which radiate like an electric fox or squirrel's tail. The needles have a glossy polish, and the sunshine sifting through them makes them burn with silvery luster, while their number and elastic temper tell delightfully in the winds.

"There are many variable arching forms, alone or in groups, with innumerable tassels drooping beneath the arches or radiant above them, and many lowly giants of no particular form that have braved the storms of a thousand years."

—John Muir in *The Mountains of California* (1894)

On the foxtail pine

"On account of its conical trunk, short branches, and short dense masses of needles Foxtail Pine shows obvious relation in its architectural form to the extreme temperature conditions and high winds of its habitat and thus lends striking interest to the isolated colonies in the high granite country, particularly in the southern Sierra Nevada."

—Willis Linn Jepson in *The Trees of California* (1923)

On the Rocky Mountain bristlecone pine

"Little is known of the extreme age attained by this species. It is believed, however, to be moderately long-lived. Trees from 16 to 20 inches in diameter are from 200 to 250 years old."

—George B. Sudworth in *The Pine Trees of the Rocky Mountain Region* (1917)

CHAPTER 3
Living a Long Life

OF THE THREE SPECIES OF FOXTAIL PINE, only Great Basin bristlecone pine has a strong public image: that of a great mass of twisted, gnarly limbs supported by a short, thick trunk lacking most of its bark and anchored to a rock outcropping. One can imagine a tree having this battered appearance after enduring hostile mountain spirits for a millennium or more. But a tree looks like that only in the final stage of a long life. Before it reaches that point it must go through three less picturesque stages.

The first stage of any tree is the seedling; the second, the sapling; next, the mature, or middle-aged, tree; and finally the tottering oldster. These stages partly follow calendar age, but they mainly follow phenotype—the visible characteristics they present to us. The phenotype results from the environment acting on an organism's genetic qualities—its genotype—so it combines information about both. The phenotype is plastic, in the sense of developing differently under different conditions.

This chapter presents a new way of looking at a tree's stages of growth in that they are described so as to be visually identifiable and they are assigned biological roles. The following descriptions of phenotypes of the four growth stages assume that the trees have been subjected throughout their lives to fairly similar conditions. By viewing these life stages in order, we can see how any one tree would progress through a long life. Except where otherwise stated, the descriptions in this chapter pertain specifically to Great Basin bristlecone pine.

The Seedling: Securing a Foothold

Foxtail pine seeds must be exposed to the chill of winter to be able to germinate when spring comes. That is a common behavioral pattern for the conifers of wintry climates, including such neighbors as the firs, spruces, and pines that share foxtail pine's habitats. But both bristlecones follow a different drummer. Their seeds are able to germinate as soon as they are shed from their cones, in September or October. At that time the soil is dry, and it would seem a poor time to begin growth. In this case, the ability to germinate may not correlate with the act of germination, as Forest Service researcher Gil Schubert reported germination of Rocky Mountain bristlecone in Arizona's San Francisco Peaks to occur after July rains. No observations have been reported of the timing of germination of Great Basin bristlecone seeds.

For all three Foxtail Pines, warm spring temperatures energize enzymes that break down the nutritive tissue that fills the seed cavity—fats into fatty acids, proteins into amino acids, and carbohydrates into soluble sugars. These nutrients feed the embryo for only a matter of days. At this stage the embryo is a tiny yellowish rod embedded in the nutritive tissue—a miniature stem

GREAT BASIN BRISTLECONE PINE SEEDLING GROWING FROM A CRACK IN A DOLOMITE BOULDER, WHITE MOUNTAINS, CALIFORNIA. —*Photo by the author*

MANY SIERRA NEVADA FOXTAIL PINE SEEDLINGS AND SAPLINGS
SHARE THE FAR SLOPE WITH OLDER TREES AT TIMBER GAP,
SEQUOIA NATIONAL PARK, CALIFORNIA. —*Photo by David Lanner*

with a primordial root at one end and a tuft of tiny needles (the cotyledons) at the other. Soon the embryo's root grows through the end of the splitting seed coat, and the cotyledons are pulled by growth of the stem into sunlight. With photosynthesis now possible, the newly launched seedling absorbs the remaining nutritive tissue and starts making its own.

At this stage, only the keenest observers will find the new seedling growing from the soil, because it is tiny and easily hidden by even the thinnest cover of rocks, plants, and other debris. Look for a 1-inch-tall reddish stem topped by a group of 5 to 7 1-inch-long green cotyledons radiating like the ribs of an umbrella. For the next few years the stem grows a few inches and has flat single needles. It will branch, thicken its stem, and finally grow needles bunched in fives. It will slowly build its woody frame and foliage mass as it establishes itself firmly into its place in the woodland.

The seedling stage is a risky time for a pine tree, and mortality rates are high. Those that survive may keep from drying out in the hot summer sun by growing in partial shade or in microtopography that retains moisture. It is said that Great Basin bristlecone pines in the White Mountains survive best on a soil of dolomite because that fractured white limestone reflects sunlight well, remaining cool and moist. Or perhaps successful seedlings are those that have been overlooked by damping-off fungi, browsing pocket gophers, or cutworm larvae, or have been fortunate enough to encounter mycorrhizal fungi in the soil.

Bill Critchfield grew seedlings of the three Foxtail species for three years before they regularly produced five-needled fascicles. He found that foxtail pine seedlings handily outgrew both bristlecones. The bristlecones "resembled cushion plants, lacking an emergent leader," while the foxtail seedlings had leaders with well-developed buds.

It is arbitrary to define the end of the seedling stage simply in terms of either height or age for any tree. Edmund Schulman found a 3-foot Great Basin bristlecone to be seven hundred years old. Anything that old is no seedling. I once knew a five-year-old eucalyptus that was 93 feet tall. Nothing that tall is a seedling either. Can we say a pine leaves the seedling stage when it is producing needles in fascicles rather than single juvenile needles? Singleleaf pinyon pines can make only juvenile (nonfascicled) needles for thirty years or more. A modest suggestion: A seedling is a tree small enough to pull up without breaking a sweat. But however we define it, one thing is clear: the most crucial task of any tree is simply securing a foothold wherever it takes root. If it succeeds in doing that, a long life becomes a possibility.

The Sapling: Reaching for the Sky

If a seedling is an infant, a sapling is a youth. A sapling must penetrate the space above it, capturing its place in the sun. It must send invading roots into unoccupied soil. If it succeeds in enlarging the foothold it gained as a seedling, it may live and thrive to maturity.

The sapling has some advantages, especially if it has an arrow-straight leading shoot forming big buds full of embryonic needles and rapidly gaining height. A vigorous young tree like this exerts in its upper parts considerable hormonal dominance over the rest of the tree, giving it a slender form with densely needled limbs.

THE CLASSIC FORM OF A GREAT BASIN BRISTLECONE PINE SAPLING,
LIKE THIS ONE IN THE WHITE MOUNTAINS, CALIFORNIA,
GIVES NO HINT OF WHAT CHANGES LIE AHEAD. —*Photo by the author*

Branches are few and they tend to reach out, densely clothed in green and supple enough to flex in strong winds. The bands of sapwood the tree forms annually during the sapling stage are the widest it forms in its life. Seed production is not yet a priority, so little energy is wasted on such sexual frivolity as making cones and pollen.

The sapling has a relatively safe life. Its phloem is too thin to offer much nutrition to bark beetles. Its slim silhouette and flexibility save it from windthrow (uprooting by wind), snow loads, and wind breakage. It has not yet lived enough years to have suffered many injuries that might invite rots, and it has witnessed few fires.

A successful sapling will eventually fill out its lanky frame. It will make many more limbs and fatten its trunk to support the more ample crown it must take to maturity. Bark thickens, cones begin to appear in large numbers, and the tree eventually moves to its next stage.

Maturity: Attaining the Evolutionary Goal

After a few hundred years, our sapling becomes a mature, or middle-aged, tree. Big branches carry masses of foliage as well as seed cones and pollen cones, much of it on fine branchlets of interfoliar origin. This is the most actively reproductive stage, and it can be argued that whatever comes after is irrelevant, because this is the phenotype that leaves the vast majority of progeny. The leader dies and is replaced by weak shoots growing in all directions, rounding or flattening the crown and guaranteeing the tree will grow no taller. The death of the leader often results in a spike of dead wood projecting above the live crown. In some trees, branches no longer in the thrall of a dominating leader sweep up to mimic it, creating pitchfork silhouettes.

As the tree becomes taller, its topmost shoots get further from their water source and leave the relatively safe boundary layer of earth and atmosphere to enter a windier, drier place. This increases water loss, reduces photosynthesis, and stunts the growth of buds high in the tree. Even coast redwoods are height-limited by moisture stress in their tops, so it is no surprise that bristlecones on droughty sites should also have limits. Stressed Great Basin bristlecone and foxtail pines may have their tops attacked and killed by the bark beetle *Pityogenes fossifrons*.

Gravity pulls lengthened branches downward, and this is countered by an upward force on branches and leaning trunks caused by the formation of denser and darker wood on the lower surface. The bulkier crown of a larger tree creates a larger wind profile. Resulting wind stress and sway stimulate the growth of compression wood—dense wood that exerts an upward pressure—lower on the trunk, where it is most needed to stabilize the tree.

Trees exposed to a constant prevailing wind on high summits or passes may become "wind trained." They lean, and their branches point downwind, offering a diminished profile that makes them less susceptible to wind damage. The blast of soil and ice particles keeps their bark thin and kills buds that attempt to grow on windward surfaces. Rocky Mountain bristlecone pine displays this trained appearance on Windy Ridge in Colorado (see photo on page 11).

A MATURE SIERRA NEVADA FOXTAIL PINE HAS MANY YEARS
OF MIDDLE AGE TO LOOK FORWARD TO AT TIMBER GAP,
SEQUOIA NATIONAL PARK, CALIFORNIA. —Photo by David Lanner

The most extreme form of wind training is the reduction of the tree to a low, bushy mat, or krummholz, at the upper tree line. This occurs with Great Basin bristlecone pine on Nevada's Mount Washington, although it is actually a rarity in this species, which grows upright at almost 12,000 feet in the White Mountains. Foxtail pine is reported to form krummholz above Red Lake in

A KRUMMHOLZ PLANT OF GREAT BASIN BRISTLECONE PINE ON MOUNT WASHINGTON IN GREAT BASIN NATIONAL PARK, NEVADA. THE PREVAILING WIND IS FROM THE RIGHT. —*Photo by the author*

the southern Sierra Nevada. There have been no reports of Rocky Mountain bristlecone pine forming krummholz.

Maturity exposes trees to centuries of insults. Fires kill or damage them by scorching their crowns, cooking their shallow roots, or destroying their cambium. Porcupines girdle the bark off trunks, killing everything above the wound. Bark beetles lay their eggs in galleries excavated under the bark so their larvae will be positioned to feed on the tree's phloem. Wood decay fungi enter infection courts opened by mechanical damage to roots, trunks, or limbs caused by lightning, wind breakage, tree falls, or rock slides. Dead limbs and trunks are bleached by the sun, cracked in freeze-thaw cycles, buffeted in the wind, pulled down by gravity, and mined by wood borers and carpenter ants. Dead wood piles up on the ground as the tree slowly slips into old age, and spacing between trees becomes wider as mortality thins the stand.

There has been a misconception that fungal and insect pests are unknown to Great Basin bristlecone pine because they cannot abide its dense, resinous wood. That isn't so. The wood of Great Basin bristlecone is indeed dense, hard, and slow to decay even on the ground, but nothing lasts forever.

Old Age: A Time of Retreat

Great Basin bristlecones that reach old age—say a thousand years or so—are unlikely to still have living tops. The broken stubs of their trunks have been dried in the wind, cracked by frost, and eroded by windborne rock and ice particles. Typically, a short, thick trunk supports masses of dense foliage borne on epicormic branches, and the dead portion of the upper trunk protrudes above the living crown. Main roots, exposed to the sun by centuries of soil erosion, clutter the ground with dead wood. Fine roots have spent centuries mining the same soil mass for nutrients and may have experienced mineral famine. These old trees have wildly individualistic appearances that attract a worldwide following of reverent visitors. For many people, the word *bristlecone* evokes dramatic images of trees in this final stage of life.

But there is more to be learned from these old conifers than platitudes about overcoming adversity. Studies of aging in Great Basin bristlecone pine have found, remarkably, that evidence of senescence—a degenerative aging process leading to death— seems nowhere to be found. In other words, unlike us humans who need bifocals as we age, whose hair loses its pigmentation, and whose ability to reproduce is systematically undermined, the essential functions of Great Basin bristlecone pine show no signs of deteriorating with age. In the 1990s, Kristina Connor and I looked for evidence of senescence by comparing some biological features of young and old Great Basin bristlecones. We chose features that had been hypothetically implicated in tree senescence by earlier researchers, and we put their hypotheses to the test.

We found that tracheids that were formed by the cambium of an ancient Great Basin bristlecone were no different in diameter than those formed in the very same tree when it was young. Diameters varied, but their trend was random, not age-related. An earlier researcher had found the same to be true of tracheid length. Nor did tree age affect the number of annual rings that made up the sapwood, or how long ray cells lived, or how many inner bark

GREAT BASIN BRISTLECONE PINES DEFY REASON BY SHOWING NO SIGNS OF
SENESCENCE IN OLD AGE. WHITE MOUNTAINS, CALIFORNIA. —*Photo by David Lanner*

cells were formed by the cambium each year. If these parameters were to degrade merely as a function of tree age, they could limit longevity by restricting the transport of water or nutrients within the tree, starving or dehydrating it, as some earlier researchers had postulated. But the cambium appears to remain young indefinitely, making functional cells for thousands of years.

We also tested whether tree longevity is limited by the accumulation of mutations. It is logical to expect that trees growing at high elevations, where they are most subject to ionizing radiation (cosmic rays), would suffer fatal DNA damage over many years. Indeed, this has been a leading hypothesis on what limits tree age. But we found no evidence that aging was correlated with mutational damage. The number of recognizable mutations in seedlings grown from the seed of young or ancient trees, the vitality of pollen, seed weight, the ability of seeds to germinate, and the growth rates of seedling offspring all were unaffected by long exposure to radiation. Our seed germination results supported earlier reports by Frits Went and by LeRoy and Jean Johnson, who found high germination rates in seeds plucked from Great Basin bristlecones several thousand years old.

Our investigations on trees aged 23 to more than 4,700 years also found no evidence of aging in the formation and growth of buds containing needles, contradicting another old speculation about age limitation in trees. This absence of an aging effect in the shoot apexes and cambium of Great Basin bristlecone pine, and the lack of impairment of its ability to reproduce successfully at an advanced age, can only raise questions over concepts of aging long used in forestry, horticulture, and dendrochronology.

DIMENSIONS

The tallest recorded tree of the three Foxtail Pine species is a 135-foot-tall foxtail pine measured by Frank Callahan in 2006. But *tallest* does not necessarily mean *largest*. American Forests, an organization that promotes healthy forest ecosystems, maintains a national register of big trees, which is updated annually. They use a point system in determining the largest tree of each species, so the listed dimensions are not necessarily the tallest, the thickest, or the widest spreading of any tree of that species, but rather a synthesis of all three. Here are the record holders of the three species of the Foxtail Pine group as of 2005:

FOXTAIL PINE
Height: 76 feet
Circumference at 4.5 feet above the ground: 316 inches
Average crown spread: 34 feet
Location: Shasta-Trinity National Forest, California

ROCKY MOUNTAIN BRISTLECONE PINE
Height: 72 feet
Circumference at 4.5 feet above the ground: 138 inches
Average crown spread: 33 feet
Location: Colfax County, New Mexico

GREAT BASIN BRISTLECONE PINE
Height: 52 feet
Circumference at 4.5 feet above the ground: 455 inches
Average crown spread: 44 feet
Location: Humboldt-Toiyabe National Forest, Nevada

Gerontologists have classified Great Basin bristlecone pine as an organism of "negligible senescence." Similar conclusions were drawn by Douglas Larson, who studied arborvitae trees (Thuja occidentalis) in Ontario up to about 1,600 years of age.

Finally, studies made by Barry Flanary and Gunther Kletetschka have shown that old Great Basin bristlecone pine chromosomes do not show marked shortening of their telomeres, or tips, as they age. Telomere shortening has been regarded as a possible cause of senescence in organisms, so its absence in bristlecones supports Connor and Lanner's findings of negligible senescence. Old trees have much to contribute to the biological study of aging.

A NEWLY MATURE GREAT BASIN BRISTLECONE PINE IN
GREAT BASIN NATIONAL PARK, NEVADA. —*Photo by the author*

CHAPTER 4

Shapes and Forms

WHEN BRISTLECONES AND FOXTAILS GROW in benign environments, as sometimes happens, they develop as tall, straight, single-stemmed trees, similar in form to the timber-producing pines familiar to us all. But the assaults they suffer in their harsh mountain homes modify their appearance, often in radical ways.

Equipped with an understanding of how these trees grow and respond to their surroundings, we can make reasoned guesses at why they look the way they do, and how they assume sometimes remarkable shapes and forms. Much of the distinctive appearance of bristlecones and foxtails can be attributed to such phenomena as sectored architecture, bark strips, leaning and twisted trunks, multiple trunks, colorful sapwood, and asymmetrical crowns.

Sectored Architecture

The bristlecone and foxtail pines appear to have a sectorial pattern of water conduction. This means that water coming up a big root moves into the trunk sector above it, with little or no diffusion to left or right, and is then distributed to the branches of that sector. So, if a big root dies, the trunk sector it formerly supplied with water will dry out and will also die, and so will the branches emanating from that sector. Presumably, the death of a crown sector, as through a bark beetle attack, could send a wave of mortality down into a sector's roots as well. This view implies that a tree may not be an individual entity as we ordinarily think of it, but rather a composite of partial trees, each expressing a degree of autonomy.

Sectored architecture has also been identified in some other western American conifers, in broad-leaved trees in New England, and in millennium-old arborvitae in Ontario, but few foresters and botanists are aware of it because it has not been identified until recently. In Holland, elms growing along a canal up which salt water had intruded in a storm had dead foliage, but only above the roots on the canal side of the tree. Sectored architecture is also apparent in stumps of felled conifers that have a root grafted to a living tree; only the sector directly above the root graft continues to live.

Sectored architecture may affect the distribution of nutrients and water in the tree's crown, and it appears to be worthy of a lot more research. Many of the most dramatic Great Basin bristlecones are composed of brightly colored dead trunk sectors, their sapwood glowing amber in the sunlight, on one side of a tree, with the other side covered by living bark and bearing dense masses of green foliage. There are unforgettable views along the Methuselah Walk, in the Schulman Grove of California's Ancient Bristlecone Pine Forest, where one can look across a canyon at Great Basin

IN THE GARDEN

The three species of Foxtail Pine have not yet found a prominent place among domesticated conifers in botanical gardens, arboreta, front and backyards, or the collections of hobbyists. This is unfortunate because the unique look of their branchlets, their compact and shiny needles, and the bright coloring of their pollen and seed cones make for interesting and unusual specimens.

Foxtail and bristlecone pines are hardy in USDA Hardiness Zones 4 through 7, and they tolerate full sun. Great Basin bristlecones are reputed to be slow growing and are recommended for potting or bonsai cultivation. A Rocky Mountain bristlecone that the author grew in Zone 4 typically added about 8 inches in height annually and grew to about 15 feet in height with a 15-foot spread in twenty-five years. Conifer enthusiasts wishing to grow these trees from seed should remember that while the bristlecones can be germinated right off the tree, foxtail pine seed should be stratified—stored in cool, moist sand—for forty-five to ninety days. The following cultivars have been named:

GREAT BASIN BRISTLECONE PINE
'Formal Form': slow growing, with very dense foliage

ROCKY MOUNTAIN BRISTLECONE PINE
'Joe's Best': conical in shape, compact in form
'Rezek Doll': similar to 'Joe's Best', but
   with a more open appearance
'Sherwood Compact': compact and
   conical with ascending branches
'Cecilia': a dwarf

FOXTAIL PINE
'Horseshoe Pillar': conical and compact, from
   subspecies *austrina*
'Dwarf Form': also known as 'Nana'

bristlecone pines marching up the slope, their woody skeletons exposed on the downhill sides and leafy branches spreading from their uphill sides. This pattern is due to the death of downhill-side roots by soil erosion, followed by sector death above the dead roots, while the uphill sides remain rooted and alive.

Bark Strips

Many tree watchers have commented on the narrow strips of bark on foxtails and bristlecones, with cambium and wood underneath, connecting a live branch to a live root along an otherwise dead trunk. These were colorfully dubbed "life lines" by Edmund Schulman, who rightly attributed them to the dying back of the cambium on both sides of the live strip. What caused the dieback?

The architecture of bristlecones suggests that the dead areas of the trunk are sectors whose roots died after exposure through soil erosion. The surviving bark strip is just a sector that has not yet died. If the bark strip's foliage or roots are killed, the strip will die. Otherwise the strip will keep adding new annual rings, year after year, growing slowly thicker but no wider. That little portion of surviving tree can look extravagantly healthy, bearing lustrous green foliage and even some seed cones. But however lush it appears, the sole surviving bark strip is nothing more than an old tree's swan song, a sign of life on borrowed time.

Strangely, the sapwood of bark strips is almost twice as thick as that of full-barked younger trees (comparison of 1,000-year-olds versus 200-year-olds). According to Kristina Connor, the younger trees' sapwood averaged 19.3 millimeters in depth, and the old bark strips' sapwood averaged 33.2 millimeters. This suggests

A 1,500-YEAR-OLD GREAT BASIN BRISTLECONE PINE AT MAMMOTH CREEK, UTAH. EXPOSURE OF ITS ROOT SYSTEM HAS KILLED ALL THE SECTORS BUT ONE AND A PORTION OF A SECOND, LEAVING LIVE BARK STRIPS. —*Photo by the author*

that bark strips deliver more water per unit of circumference than do intact trees, which would seem to be a happy circumstance for the foliage they support.

Leaning Trunks

A tree's natural tendency is to grow upright, but there are several factors that can cause any tree to lean. Soil or snow creep may push it slowly downhill, causing the stem to lean in that direction. Or the tree may throw out more branches on one side than on the other, making it lean in the direction of the heavier side. Commonly, a tree will begin life shaded on one side by another tree. The new tree will grow toward the light and lean away from the larger neighbor. This is a hormonally mediated behavior that usually ensures a better-lighted future for the younger tree. Leaning may also be caused by loss of soil under one side of a tree, usually due to erosion.

A leaning reaction quite common among Great Basin bristlecone pines sometimes occurs when two trees begin life at about the same time and within a few feet of each other. Apparently, close company is not good company, and by the time they are mature their trunks lean sharply away from each other, forming a pronounced V. The inside of the V is usually devoid of branches almost to the top.

Leans are usually limited by a tree's attempts to straighten and "verticalize" itself. Growth hormones in the cambium of a leaning stem migrate to the stem's lower side, stimulating the wood growth there. This compression wood exerts the pushing force that prevents the lean from getting steeper.

Twisted Stems

Rarely, Great Basin bristlecones have trunks or major branches that look like a thick rope of spiraling strands. Images of one such tree have found their way into at least two books, a calendar, a tote bag, a Web site, a T-shirt, and a magazine article. An observer may infer about such a shape that the stem has actually been physically twisted. Some have attributed this morphology to strong winds that force a tree into this shape by exerting torque, but no evidence has been presented to support such a possibility. Based on the sectored growth of Great Basin bristlecone pine, I suggest that

A LONG-DEAD GREAT BASIN BRISTLECONE PINE IN THE WHITE MOUNTAINS, CALIFORNIA, SHOWING THE PRONOUNCED SPIRAL GRAIN AND SECTORED ARCHITECTURE THAT GIVE IT A TWISTED APPEARANCE. —*Photo by Amadej Trnkoczy*

the twisted look is caused by disproportionate cambial growth along one of the sectors of a stem with strongly spiral grain. This accounts for the phenomenon in the simplest way, without requiring heroic behavior on the part of the tree.

Multiple Trunks

Unlike foxtails and Rocky Mountain bristlecones, which usually grow as single stems, Great Basin bristlecones often grow in clumps of two or more stems joined at the base. Are these multiple forks of a single tree, or are they separate tree trunks, grown from seeds that sprouted very close together and fused at the base? Or have they arisen from seedlings like "cushion plants," lacking a central leader and putting up several equal branches as trunk substitutes? The answer can be very hard to determine, especially with trees that have had many centuries to grow into shapes that obscure their origins.

A pine can generate multiple trunks through injury. A seedling's leader can be killed early in life, allowing two or more branches to sweep upward as replacement leaders. These new leaders may retain a curve at the point where they began to grow vertically, or they may straighten up over time. Numerous bushy Great Basin bristlecones, up to 3 feet or so in height, can be seen in the Patriarch Grove in the White Mountains. They lack a distinctive dominant leader and may represent an early stage of multiple-stemmed trees.

Another way a pine can generate multiple trunks is through the death of the leading bud before it or the side buds ever grow out as woody branches. The side buds then grow out into near-vertical replacement leaders of about equal size. The kind of steep forks that this leads to are common in Great Basin bristlecone as well as in other conifers (for example, lodgepole pine, whitebark pine, and limber pine).

Edmund Schulman surmised that his ancient tree Methuselah, usually described as the oldest living tree, developed its present form when its single trunk died, stimulating the upward growth of a low limb. Two more repetitions of this process produced what Schulman called the "pickaback" form, one trunk of which still lives. This phenomenon has not been analyzed in the years since Schulman's writing.

Another way to get a multiple-trunked tree is by knocking a tree down. If some of its roots remain alive and in the ground, the branches, no longer inhibited by the dominating leader, grow rapidly upward like little "treelets." If the fallen trunk rests on soil that remains moist from a heavy snowpack, or from sediment washed up against it by overland flow from rainstorms, then roots can grow from it at various places along its length. In some trees this can encourage the sprouting of roots along the fallen trunk, although that has never been documented with a bristlecone or foxtail—at least not yet. This process, a form of layering, occurs in some tropical trees and in coast redwood. I have also seen it in a cottonwood, a maple, and an alder. Two white pines—whitebark pine and Japanese stone pine (*Pinus pumila*)—are known to form such roots in nature.

Bristlecones do, however, put up erect treelets from fallen trees. I have seen this occur on fallen trees on Mount Washington, Nevada, and along the Methuselah Walk in the White Mountains,

California. This leads to a clone of tree trunks arranged in a line. Eventually the fallen trunk could decay, leaving each new tree on its own roots. Those roots and the lower portions of the trunks could fuse if they remain in contact with each other.

Truly multiple trunks—that is, trunks that each grew from a separate seed—can result from the random arrival of seeds very close to each other on the ground, or their deliberate placement in the soil by an animal. All three species of the Foxtail Pine group have winged seeds that are adapted to wind dispersal and that fall randomly on the ground. For several seeds to land within inches of each other, to survive predators actively seeking them,

BRANCHES OF A FALLEN GREAT BASIN BRISTLECONE PINE GROWING AS "TREELETS." —Photo by the author

70

to germinate, and to mature as a clump of stems must be a low-probability event.

Seed dispersal by animals, however, can lead to a very different outcome. Clark's nutcracker inhabits the home ranges of all three species of Foxtail. They hide seeds an inch or two underground, mostly singly, but often in groups of up to a dozen or so. Seeds that are not retrieved and eaten as winter food, or fed to baby nutcrackers, can germinate. Therefore, pines dispersed by nutcrackers can have a high frequency of multiple-stemmed clumps.

If multiple trunks in a clump are blown down by wind, exposing their root systems, their individuality becomes obvious. But if we can only see what is above ground, it is difficult to tell whether a clump of stems represents individual trees on their own roots, or a single tree that has made multiple trunks. For a definitive answer, genetic analysis of enzymes known as isozymes can be performed. The identification of more than one genotype (individual) in a stem clump would mean the stems are from separate seeds, while the presence of only one genotype would mean the stems originated from a single seed.

Genetic analyses by forest geneticists Seok-Woo Lee, Thomas Ledig, and David Johnson have shown the great majority of multitrunked Great Basin bristlecones in their study areas in the White Mountains to be single trees with multiple forks, probably resulting from physical injury when young. Fewer clumps are made up of genetically different individuals due to the caching of seeds, probably by nutcrackers. The full contribution of nutcrackers to bristlecone reproduction, however, can only be learned by knowing how many of the single-stemmed trees grew

THE PATRIARCH

Since it was first brought to the public's attention in Edmund Schulman's 1958 *National Geographic Magazine* article, the Patriarch bristlecone in the White Mountains has been described as the largest Great Basin bristlecone pine. It consists of six major trunks and about three smaller ones, forming a small grove 20 feet long and about 38 feet in circumference. Some of the trunks are upright; others lean outward. The bases of the major roots have been exposed by soil erosion, and in several cases they have fused together to form a pedestal of alternating living and dead areas.

I wrote in my 1984 book *Trees of the Great Basin* that the Patriarch "is not one tree but at least one clump containing seven or perhaps nine trees from seeds in one or more nutcracker caches. Where the trunks touch each other they grow together and appear as one." But I was never happy with that conclusion, and in 1988 I persuaded Professor Yan Linhart of the University of Colorado to analyze in his lab the isozymes of foliage from several trunks. Joan Benner and Carole Gerard of the Inyo National Forest clipped branchlets from six separate trunks on two occasions and shipped them to Colorado for analysis. Both tests showed unequivocally that the Patriarch is, in Linhart's words, "a single patriarch and not just a bunch of good ole boys." In other words, the stems are all genetically identical, parts of the same individual tree. A decade later, Tom Ledig arrived at a similar conclusion.

How did a single tree grow into such a multitrunked monstrosity in its estimated 1,500 years? I suggest it was converted by adventitious rooting from a single fallen tree into a small clone. This could only have happened during a moist period when soil became dammed up against the fallen trunk and remained wet long enough for roots to form. We will never know for sure until the Patriarch is carefully dissected, and nobody can say when that will happen.

THE BASE OF THE PATRIARCH IN THE WHITE MOUNTAINS, CALIFORNIA,
SHOWING ITS MULTIPLE TRUNKS AND SEVERAL LIVE
AND DEAD SECTORS. —*Photo by the author*

from cached seeds. This would be difficult to ascertain, as it would require marking the position of cached single seeds and observing their germination and growth.

Colorful Sapwood

The three Foxtail cousins put on beautiful displays of color all year. Dead snags, stumps, roots, and strips of dead wood on living trees all can develop colorful stripes along the wood grain. The palette ranges from black and gray, to reddish brown and russet, to a bright golden yellow. According to University of Minnesota forest pathologist Dr. Robert Blanchette, the stains are caused by species of wood decay fungi, white rot fungi in an early decay stage, and fungi reacting chemically with resin in the wood.

Fungal spores of several species are brought to the sapwood by bark beetles, metallic wood borers (*Buprestids*), and longhorned borers (*Cerambycids*). There they germinate and produce filaments that digest sapwood. The process of digestion is probably very slow because of the cold, dry climate, so perhaps the streaks of color we see today will still be there for the artists and photographers who will come looking for them in future centuries.

Asymmetrical Crowns

A few years ago, Mike Rourke of Palomar College made a re-markable discovery about the crowns of foxtail pine and, to a lesser degree, the two bristlecone species. Trees in the sapling stage have crowns that appear circular around the trunk when seen from above. Such crowns form a cone, with the narrow end upward. But as the sapling passes into the mature stage, the crown becomes elliptical when seen from above, with the long axis of the ellipse nearly parallel to the earth's meridian. In other words, the crowns become narrow from east to west, and considerably wider from north to south.

Some of the branches that emerge from the trees' east and west sides grow less than those that emerge from the north and south sides of the trunk—but others actually *bend* to the north or south. Prevailing winds are from the west in Foxtail habitats, so this growth pattern does not streamline the trees; in fact, it does the opposite. Like all new scientific discoveries, this one will require further study for insights on its extent and causes.

CHAPTER 5
Threats

EVERY TREE SPECIES COEXISTS WITH MANY ORGANISMS and experiences many nonbiotic factors that routinely damage or kill trees, usually in small numbers over many years, without endangering the existence of the species. Pines are notoriously vulnerable to fire, bark beetles, and rust fungi. Normally these enemies make light to moderate impacts that do not bring about local extinction. But for the three Foxtail species, the twenty-first century may mark a change in the old rules. The National Park Service now considers air pollution in Sequoia and Kings Canyon National Parks to be among the worst in the national park system. As the years pass, the mountains of western North America become less and less of a refuge for high-elevation conifers. New diseases, invigorated insect pests, and changes in climate and atmosphere endanger species that have evolved in conditions now irrevocably changed.

Global Warming

During the twentieth century, temperatures in the western United States increased by 2 to 5 degrees Fahrenheit (1 to 3 degrees

Celsius). Warming is expected to continue in the twenty-first century at a roughly similar rate. Higher temperatures have many direct and indirect effects on a tree's biology—some favorable, others unfavorable or even dangerous.

Higher temperatures increase rates of photosynthesis, which might lead to faster growth and more food storage in a tree's tissues. But respiration rates also increase with temperature, consuming reserves that need to be conserved. The longer growing season associated with a warmer climate allows trees to become larger and to mature sooner; but it also increases vulnerability to

COPIOUS REGENERATION OF GREAT BASIN BRISTLECONE PINE
IN THE PATRIARCH GROVE, WHITE MOUNTAINS, CALIFORNIA.
AN EFFECT OF A WARMING CLIMATE? —*Photo by the author*

Carbon Dioxide: Friend or Foe?

The increased concentration of atmospheric carbon dioxide in the last century raises questions about its effect on trees. On one hand, carbon dioxide is a greenhouse gas implicated in global warming, and warming has potentially damaging effects on high-elevation trees. On the other hand, increased carbon dioxide levels could benefit trees through a "fertilizing" effect, by providing more raw material for photosynthesis.

Some of the early research done on carbon dioxide relationships with western conifers produced evidence that Great Basin bristlecone, whitebark, and lodgepole pines (Pinus contorta), as well as mountain hemlock (Tsuga mertensiana), seemed to be responding to increased carbon dioxide with wider growth rings. But it's difficult to separate the effects of climate from those of carbon dioxide. In addition, results of that research were not supported by results of a separate study on foxtail pine. More data are needed before we can safely generalize on carbon dioxide's effects on that species.

late spring frosts or early fall frosts by starting growth too early or continuing it too late. Late frosts destroy tender tissues at the beginning of the growth cycle, while early frosts freeze tissues that have not yet hardened off. Freezes that interfere with sexual reproduction prevent normal seeds from forming, reducing the tree's ability to create another generation.

Higher temperatures are usually associated with increased drought, causing soil moisture to be in short supply and placing trees under water stress. Water-stressed trees are more susceptible to root diseases as well as insect attacks. Higher temperatures also increase winter rainfall at the cost of snowfall at high elevations, leaving trees without sufficient moisture from snowmelt in the spring and summer. In California, for instance, the time it takes for snow on the ground to melt decreased by sixteen days between 1951 and 1996.

Theoretically, trees with wind-borne seeds should be able to escape some of the effects of warming by migrating to higher, cooler habitats. But the foxtail and bristlecone pines already occupy a narrow elevational band at or near the tree line, so there is hardly anywhere to go for refuge. Thus they would find themselves stressed by a climate different from what they have experienced in their recent evolutionary past, and to which they might not be able to adapt.

Forest Fires

Fire has been only a moderate threat to the three Foxtail cousins in the past. They grow in relatively fire-resistant habitats low in combustible woody fuels. Many of their stands are made up of scattered trees too far apart to pass fire from one to another or without a dense ground cover of combustible brush. But warming will bring drying, and dry fuels burn hotter and more rapidly. Warming also subjects pines to water stress, which invites bark beetle attack and results in more dead trees, increasing fuel volumes. The fire threat will be most severe at the lower edges of these forests, where fires burning in stands of other species become a source of ignitions, and fire winds from downslope make greater inroads into open woodlands.

GREAT BASIN BRISTLECONE PINE SHOWING A SECTOR KILLED BY FIRE DAMAGE TO A MAJOR ROOT, AND SIGNS OF BARK BEETLE AND WOOD BORER ACTIVITY. MAMMOTH CREEK, DIXIE NATIONAL FOREST, UTAH. —*Photo by the author*

Bark Beetles

The most dangerous insect pest attacking the foxtail and bristle-cones is a bark beetle called the mountain pine beetle (*Dendroctonus ponderosae*). The adult female bores through the bark of the trunk in the summer, excavating a vertical gallery along which she lays her eggs. In a successful attack, fertilized eggs produce legless larvae, which feed on phloem tissue, disrupting the flow of carbohydrates and other substances to the roots. At the same time, blue stain fungi brought into the tree by the adult beetles proliferate in the sapwood, clogging it and depriving the crown of water. Heavy infestations are often fatal and affect many trees over large areas.

Fortunately for most foxtail and bristlecone pines, mountain pine beetles breed slowly at cool, high altitudes; two years are needed for a new generation of adults to emerge. This subjects the developing beetles to two harsh winters and keeps their populations in check. But with global warming, the generation period shortens to one year. This has already occurred, devastatingly, in Rocky Mountain stands of whitebark pine. Adding insult to injury, groups of dead pines killed by beetles dramatically raise the risk of fire.

White Pine Blister Rust

The story of white pine blister rust is a tragedy well-known to North American naturalists and biologists. The fungus that causes this often-fatal disease is *Cronartium ribicola*. It must spend part of its life cycle on gooseberry and currant bushes (the genus *Ribes*)—and then it can spread to five-needled white pines. This host requirement does not protect the white pines, because gooseberries and currants are common in western conifer forests. For example, in California's White Mountains, three species of *Ribes* grow in the pinyon-juniper forest just below the zone where Great Basin bristlecones live, and one species grows among the bristlecones.

Once a pine's needles are infected, the fungal strands grow down into the branches, killing them and destroying their ability to produce seed crops. With multiple branch infections, the tree dies. Since it was introduced from Europe to Vancouver, British Columbia, in 1910 on imported white pine seedlings, white pine blister rust has ravaged forests of western white pine (*Pinus monticola*) and sugar pine (*Pinus lambertiana*) from the Pacific Coast east to the Rockies and south to the central Sierra Nevada. In the past two decades it has depleted forests of whitebark pine in the northern Rockies, especially in Glacier National Park and the Canadian Rockies. Many stands of limber pine have been attacked, and an infestation of southwestern white pine in New Mexico has raised fears of the disease spreading south into the white pine forests of Mexico.

Now it has begun to attack foxtail and bristlecone pines. The earliest report of white pine blister rust attacking foxtail pine was in the Klamath Mountains population, on Marble Mountain in 1968. It is not yet present in the Sierra Nevada population. In 2000, the disease was found for the first time in a Rocky Mountain bristlecone pine in the Sangre de Cristo Range of New Mexico. It has not yet been discovered in Great Basin bristlecone pine.

Inoculation tests performed by forest pathologists and geneticists have detected some resistance to the pathogen in both bristlecones, but foxtail pine appears to be highly susceptible. Additional cause for concern is the recent discovery that two other common genera of plants—elephant's head (*Pedicularis*) and Indian paintbrush (*Castilleja*)—can also host white pine blister rust, as *Ribes* species do. These accounts are preliminary; a great deal more study is needed before we can measure the danger posed to the three Foxtail cousins by white pine blister rust.

CHAPTER 6
Age and Longevity

FOR DECADES THE GIANT SEQUOIA (*Sequoiadendron giganteum*) was believed to live longer than any other tree, with an established age of over 3,000 years. John Muir reported 4,000 rings in a burned sequoia snag back in the nineteenth century, but the count was never confirmed and the snag never found again. Huge coast redwoods were known to be over 2,000 years old, and naturalists concluded that great age was correlated with great size attained on rich, well-watered soils.

Edmund Schulman found exceptions to this rule in the 1940s while exploring the Rocky Mountains for very old trees that could provide long tree-ring records. Such records are obtained by boring the tree with an increment borer, a 12-to-36-inch or longer hollow-shafted drill that allows a pencil-like core to be removed from the tree. Such a core, when sanded and polished, displays latewood bands that allow one to count annual rings and closely estimate tree age—if the borer is precisely aimed into the tree's pith. To Schulman's surprise, 860-year-old trees, one a Colorado pinyon pine (*Pinus edulis*) and the other a Douglas fir (*Pseudotsuga* menziesii), were discovered in very arid sites in Colorado. But these "over-age drought conifers" did not approach the giant sequoias in age, so they did not cause much of a stir among scientists.

But in 1958, when Schulman revealed seventeen Great Basin bristlecone pines in the White Mountains to be over 4,000 years old, the landscape of biological aging suddenly changed. The extreme longevity of the bristlecones was correlated not with excellent growing conditions but with harsh conditions, like those Schulman had called attention to earlier. Great Basin bristlecones were the ultimate over-age drought conifers. Schulman suggested that giant sequoias probably had the greatest *potential* life span, because the oldest ones were still healthy and vigorous with many more years ahead of them, while the oldest bristlecones "had been dying for two millenniums or more." But the counterintuitive occurrence of ancient trees in stony subalpine drought zones reinforced in Schulman the idea that "adversity begets longevity," a view still widely accepted today. His suggestion about the potential age of giant sequoias has been largely forgotten.

Schulman's discoveries brought widespread attention to the science of dendrochronology and to his institution, the Laboratory of Tree-Ring Research at the University of Arizona in Tuscon. They also made the White Mountains of California famous, and they led directly to the establishment of the Ancient Bristlecone Pine Forest within the Inyo National Forest.

The Oldest Living—and Dead— Bristlecone Pines

The oldest trees are Great Basin bristlecone pines, so the rest of this chapter will focus on that species. Schulman named the oldest bristlecone pine he found Methuselah and pronounced it the "world's oldest known living thing." In his 1958 *National Geographic Magazine* article, Schulman gave Methuselah's age as more than 4,600 years. Years later, Tom Harlan, who joined the Laboratory of Tree-Ring Research weeks after Schulman's death, discovered that Schulman had taken his cores at breast height (4.5 feet above the ground, as foresters do) and that he had added 200 years for the tree to attain that height. So it is probable that Schulman actually counted about 4,400 rings in Methuselah. Schulman stated that missing rings made precise dating impossible, but his coring method would also have introduced imprecisions because of the arbitrariness of his 200-year estimate.

Tom Harlan has carefully analyzed cores taken lower on the trunk of Methuselah but still well above ground level. He has dated the innermost ring to 2491 BC. When the 2007 growth ring is laid down, the innermost ring will be 4,498 years old. A more precise date could only be achieved by carefully sectioning the trunk at ground level to reveal its first seedling growth ring, which is unlikely to occur.

Today Methuselah has a living trunk reaching over 50 feet in height, and two dead ones. Its crown, supported by a single bark strip, bears healthy foliage, pollen cones, and seed cones. For some years it was identified by a sign, but to foil vandals it is no longer marked and the Forest Service guards its location from the general public.

Methuselah no longer warrants the title of "oldest known living thing." Another contribution to old-tree studies that Tom Harlan has made is the analysis of a tree that Schulman cored, but that his death left uncounted. After the passage of several decades, Harlan is uncertain whether the cores went all the way to the tree's pith, but he thinks not. Harlan's date for this tree's innermost ring is 2800 BC, so addition of the 2007 growth ring will make the innermost ring 4,806 years old, excluding an unknown number of rings before breast height was attained. This is currently the oldest known living tree. To protect this Great Basin bristlecone pine from vandals and souvenir hunters, Harlan has kept its location concealed.

Actually, the record number of years known to have been lived by any tree belongs to a Great Basin bristlecone that met its tragic end in 1964. At that time it was generally believed that all of the really old bristlecones were in California's White Mountains. But in the summer of 1964, Donald R. Currey came upon an old tree, which he designated WPN-114, on the north slope of Wheeler Peak in Nevada's Snake Range. The tree was already known to local mountaineers as "Prometheus." Currey, a University of North Carolina geologist, had been studying ice age glaciology in the moraines and cirques of Wheeler Peak, which is the only Great Basin peak outside the White Mountains to rise above 13,000 feet. There were numerous old bristlecones in his research area, and Currey decided to use their annual rings to date one of the moraines. The one hundred fourteenth tree selected for study in White Pine County was WPN-114. It attracted Currey's attention because it appeared to be "super, super old."

Standing at 10,750 feet on a ridge of glacial debris, Prometheus was mostly a massive snag of dead wood reaching 17 feet in height. A thick branch emerged 11 feet up the trunk on the north side and bore lush foliage supported by a single bark strip. At 1.5 feet above ground level, the trunk was 252 inches in circumference. As Currey related to me in 1991, he ran into some bad luck: he was unable to extract usable increment cores for ring counting, and his borer's bit broke off in the dense wood. So he asked for assistance from Humboldt National Forest district ranger Don Cox. Assistance came on August 7, 1964, in the form of a Forest Service crew that felled the tree.

Back in North Carolina, with a slab cut from the stump, Currey counted 4,844 rings. He estimated, in a 1965 paper published in *Ecology*, that Prometheus may have been 4,900 years old. A later count by Don Graybill of the Laboratory of Tree-Ring Research disclosed 4,862 rings. That figure stands as the greatest number of growth rings counted on any tree.

Currey's article citing the age of Prometheus and clinically reporting its demise created an uproar in the scientific and environmental communities, the national media, and the United States Congress. Currey and the Forest Service were severely criticized for killing the world's oldest tree. The controversy intensified with the news of a fatal heart attack suffered by Fred Solace, a Forest Service worker who had been dispatched to Wheeler Peak to clean up the old tree's debris and to bring back another stump section.

In 1987, the bristlecone forest of Wheeler Peak officially became part of the newly created Great Basin National Park. Visitors to the park can hike through the bristlecone stands below the peak, but they are not directed to the remains of old Prometheus, whose massive stump slowly decays in the rain and snow.

The question is often asked: Might there be some 5,000-year-olds still out there in the White Mountains or the Snake Range? Certainly there might be, and they could be of marginal value to dendrochronologists. But biology is not a sporting event, and finding the oldest or the biggest is of more benefit to the finder's ego than to science. Nor can we ever be certain of the maximum age attainable for a tree of any species. But humanity thrives on tales of ancient living things. Our comparatively fleeting life span of less than a century naturally leads us to ask, What is the secret of bristlecone longevity?

The Secret of Long Life

The rest of the book examines some of the issues that surround old age in trees, including a coniferous version of the age-old question of nature versus nurture. Is there something innate in Great Basin bristlecone pine that allows it to get older than other trees, or is its longevity due to its environment?

An Ancient Inheritance

The nature side of the argument gains support from the fact that Great Basin bristlecone's neighbors never live as long as it does, even though they are growing under similar conditions in the same place. The oldest known limber pine has been dated at 1,670 years. Whitebark pine has reached 1,267 years. Engelmann spruce barely exceeds 900 years. The other two Foxtail species grow older than those pines: Rocky Mountain bristlecone comes in at 2,435, and Sierra Nevada foxtail at 2,110 years. Whatever secret of long life the three Foxtail Pine species share in their genetic makeup, Great Basin bristlecone apparently has the biggest dose of it.

In a 1954 letter to *Science* that took Edmund Schulman to task for documenting ancient trees without explaining why they live so long, Forest Service tree-disease expert Willis Wagener suggested that a high resin content of the wood might be crucial in reducing wood decay. Others suggested that relative decay resistance of bristlecone wood was due to a high concentration of resin canals, making the wood itself more resin soaked—but they offered no evidence. Finally, in the 1990s, Kristina Connor compared resin canal density along 1-inch lengths of increment cores from ten Great Basin bristlecones and five limber pines. The bristlecones averaged 65.4 (with a range of 51 to 80) resin canals and the

SURVIVAL AND SURVIVABILITY

The great age of some foxtail and bristlecone pines may have genetic significance, and it could increase their chances of surviving global warming or other threats. Individuals ranging from a few decades to thousands of years of age "grew up" at different times in the past, under different environmental conditions. Each tree, depending on its age, has "sampled" a particular climate in its youth, and has been subjected to its own set of selective pressures. Therefore the population as a whole preserves what biologists Ronald Hiebert and James Hamrick call a "genetic memory" of past environmental variations. If global warming should severely stress these old populations, the offspring of trees that survived such conditions in the past might prove equally adapted to do so, increasing the possibility of long-term survival. On the other hand, such speculation may be little more than wishful thinking.

limber pines averaged 36.3 (with a range of 27 to 50), bolstering past speculations about resin canal density correlating with longevity. Decay-resistant wood might prolong the time before its last living sector finally breaks up under the tree's own weight.

Another pro-nature argument could be based on the results of Kristina Connor's fruitless search for signs of senescent decline in Great Basin bristlecone pine. She found no evidence of age-induced changes. One could argue that the species is extremely long-lived because it can function normally for a great many years without showing signs of senescence. But we don't know whether shorter-lived species display age-induced changes late in their lives, because they have not been subjected to similar research.

A common suggestion is that the presence of living bark strips enables old bristlecones to persist by maintaining a balance of water-procuring roots and water-consuming foliage. In other words, sectored architecture slows death by allowing a tree to linger until the last vestige finally gives up the ghost.

Finally, I suggest that the ability of all three Foxtail cousins to produce branches from their needle bundles facilitates great longevity. Every needle fascicle on these pines' leaders, and many of those on other shoots, can potentially replace the big, old branches, so vulnerable to breakage, by producing epicormic branches. Without this means of crown replacement, a tree would have to rely on its original branches to elongate annually and make new needles. Branches of the oldest trees, if they stayed alive for thousands of years, would be unable to support their own weight and would be reduced to crawling grotesquely on the ground, hundreds of feet from the mother tree.

All of these ideas have merit and probably play important roles in allowing bristlecones to reach extended ages. But are these factors sufficient, or does the bristlecone's environment also have a major role?

Picking the Right Neighborhood

The idea that environment controls longevity stems from Schulman's observation that in the White Mountains all of the very old Great Basin bristlecones are found at "the farthest limit of the dry forest edge, [on] outcroppings of calcareous rock, and [with] little rainfall—probably no more than 10 inches a year." Later, dendrochronologist Valmore C. LaMarche Jr. pointed out that the necessary level of aridity to create "old-age habitat" could come about not only from low precipitation, but from high evaporation rates, shallow soils, location near the crest of a ridge, and other climatic, soil, and physiographic factors. Prometheus, for example, grew in a relatively moist region but was located on a ridge of permeable rocky material that held very little water.

Why would bristlecones live longer in places where they could barely survive? Some years ago I compared the occurrence of potential mortality factors in two Great Basin bristlecone groves— one at a mild low-elevation site, and the other high on a cold, windy mountain. The mild site in my study was a mixed conifer forest above Mammoth Creek in southern Utah's Dixie National Forest. Great Basin bristlecones grow here at about 8,000 feet among tall white firs (Abies concolor), ponderosa pines, and even an occasional Colorado pinyon pine. The presence of those conifers

GREAT BASIN BRISTLECONE PINES GROWING WITH PONDEROSA PINES AT 8,000
FEET, IN THE MILD ENVIRONMENT OF MAMMOTH CREEK IN UTAH'S DIXIE
NATIONAL FOREST, HAVE NOT EXCEEDED 1,500 YEARS. —*Photo by the author*

immediately suggests a mild climate. The bristlecones grow tall and straight, up to 70 feet in height and 30 inches in diameter in 275 years—growth that usually correlates with deep soils rich in organic material. The oldest bristlecone on this site was a 1,500-year-old, 20-foot-tall tree with most of its roots exposed by soil erosion.

The higher, colder, and windier site was a grove of old trees at 10,500 feet on Wheeler Peak, Nevada, growing with bushy Engelmann spruces, prostrate common junipers (*Juniperus communis*), and an occasional limber pine. The bristlecones, several of them 3,000 years old or more, reach about 25 feet in height and have diameters up to 50 inches. They are scattered among quartzite boulders with pockets of thin soil between.

At Mammoth Creek, the lower trunks of several bristlecones had numerous pitch tubes, 0.75-inch-wide masses of congealed resin formed by resin flow from bark beetle bore holes. The Wheeler Peak site had no such evidence of bark beetle attack. Other Mammoth Creek trunk injuries, not seen on Wheeler Peak, were rows of sapsucker holes around the circumference of several bristlecones, forming a zone of physical weakness in the wood, and dead tops due to girdling of the stem by porcupines feeding on inner bark.

But most significantly, at Mammoth Creek numerous bristlecones had "cat faces"—fire scars extending from the ground several feet up the trunk—and charred wood where roots joined the base of the tree. This evidence was left by repeated ground fires, with associated wood decay. At the Wheeler Peak site I found no signs of past fires.

At 10,500 feet on Wheeler Peak, Nevada, Great Basin bristlecone pines can exceed 3,000 years under rigorous conditions. —*Photo by the author*

All this suggests that bristlecones live longer in cold, dry, high-elevation sites like those of the White Mountains and Wheeler Peak because those sites discourage bristlecone's enemies. Bark beetles, which are major killers of pines almost everywhere they grow, breed fewer generations at high altitudes where the season is short. Further, the slow growth of the pines at high altitudes may not produce enough nutritious pine phloem to support mass attacks.

At Mammoth Creek, fires have been fed by downed fir and pine logs, shed branches, and an abundance of shrubs and grasses in the openings between trees. At Wheeler Peak, the ground is covered mostly by rock and the trees are spaced more widely, greatly reducing the chance for a lightning-ignited fire to spread. The protection from fire that trees can enjoy when they are widely spaced in a rocky landscape cannot be overstated as a factor permitting great age.

There is another possibility that is on its face improbable, but not to be dismissed. Gerontologist C. E. "Tuck" Finch has made the intriguing suggestion that Clark's nutcrackers may have enabled Great Basin bristlecones to become ancient by dispersing their seeds and establishing their seedlings in harsh ground where unburied seeds perished.

So it appears that the world's oldest trees pursue a strategy of living in places where they can only barely survive and reproduce, but where their enemies fare even worse. To come back to our original query: Is exceptionally long life innate, due to genetic factors? Or is it entirely a question of environment? The answer has to be both. A hugely long life can only be realized by an individual that has the right genetic constitution, and that chooses the right neighborhood in which to put down its roots. Great Basin bristlecone pine, more than any other tree species, has the "right stuff" genetically and the good fortune to have established itself in some extraordinary western American mountains.

And what of those favored few trees that escape their adversaries and persist for millennia? What finally becomes of them? Can they live forever, and if not, what finally kills them? Ironically, they ensure their deaths by outlasting the environment that made

THE AGES ATTAINED BY THESE GREAT BASIN BRISTLECONE PINES IN DIXIE NATIONAL FOREST, UTAH, WERE LIMITED BY EROSION OF THE SOIL IN WHICH THEY WERE ROOTED. —Photo by the author

QUAKING ASPEN CLONES MAY ACHIEVE GREAT LONGEVITY BY
CONTINUALLY PRODUCING NEW SERIES OF SPROUTS FROM THE ROOTS
OF OLDER ONES. BOULDER MOUNTAIN, UTAH. —*Photo by the author*

holly's triploid characteristics have been found nearby, and these have been carbon dated at about 43,600 years. This strongly implies that a triploid bush, always a rarity, lived many years ago and has survived to the present by vegetatively propagating itself. The team of scientists who established these facts seems to have left little room for quibbling: of all the world's woody vegetables, King's holly of Tasmania has lived the longest of all.

One may protest: But these are all clones—That's not the same thing as an individual tree, is it? The difference between a clone and an individual may not be so significant. The clone starts as a seedling that puts out roots and shoots. It is, of course, an organism. New shoots sprout from its root system, some distance out from the original seedling's trunk, and they in turn put down new roots. Is this tree now less of an organism than when it consisted of only one trunk? Eventually it consists of thousands of trunks that emerge from points even further out on what becomes a very complex root system, but it is quite literally one organism.

One might argue, however, that a clone is not an individual because clones constantly replace dead parts with new growth, so that none of the tissues ever become very old. But that is also true of freestanding trees. A very old Great Basin bristlecone pine's foliage lives no more than thirty-five to forty-five years. Reproductive structures live only a year or two. The heartwood is all dead, and the oldest living cells in the sapwood are less than two hundred years old. So the old tree, too, is constantly replacing its organs and tissues.

What makes old trees different from clones is that each annual sheath of wood is wrapped around all that came before, preserving evidence of a past for us to examine. A bristlecone pine's roots, trunk, and crown develop from a seedling and stay right there on that spot of earth. When we look at one that has a thousand annual rings, we know it has spent a thousand years right there, and much of the ancient material is still there. It doesn't wander, as a clone can. It must remain stationary and resist everything the environment can throw at it. Does this not put it in a special category?

All true, and in most minds this plea probably trumps all biological reasoning. Our argument can be resolved by accepting King's holly as the longest persisting higher-plant clone, and Great Basin bristlecone pine as the longest-lived nonclonal tree.

Bibliography

Arno, Stephen F., and Ramona P. Hammerly. *Timberline: Mountain and Arctic Forest Frontiers.* Seattle: The Mountaineers, 1984.

Baas, Pieter, Rudolf Schmid, and Bertie Joan van Heuven. "Wood Anatomy of *Pinus longaeva* (Bristlecone Pine) and the Sustained Length-on-Age Increase of Its Tracheids. *IAWA Bulletin* (International Association of Wood Anatomists), new series, 7 (1986): 221–28.

Bailey, Dana K. "Phytogeography and Taxonomy of Pinus Subsection *Balfourianae.*" *Annals of the Missouri Botanical Garden* 57 (1970): 210–49.

Baker, William L. "Structure, Disturbance, and Change in the Bristlecone Pine Forests of Colorado." *Arctic and Alpine Research* 24 (1992): 17–26.

Beasley, R. S., and J. O. Klemmedson. "Ecological Relationships of Bristlecone Pine." *American Midland Naturalist* 104 (1980): 242–52.

———. "Recognizing Site Adversity and Drought-Sensitive Trees in Stands of Bristlecone Pine (*Pinus longaeva*)." *Economic Botany* 27 (1973): 141–46.

Bidartondo, M. I., J. Baar, and T. D. Bruns. "Low Ectomycorrhizal Inoculum Potential and Diversity from Soils in and near Ancient Forests of Bristlecone Pine (*Pinus longaeva*)." *Canadian Journal of Botany* 79 (2001): 293–99.

Bond, Barbara J., and Jerry F. Franklin. "Aging in Pacific Northwest Forests: A Selection of Recent Research." *Tree Physiology* 22 (2002): 73–76.

Bridges, Andrew. "Unassuming Bush May Be World's Oldest Living Thing." *Sacramento Bee*, January 30, 2002.

Brunstein, F. Craig, and David K. Yamaguchi. "The Oldest Known Rocky Mountain Bristlecone Pines (*Pinus aristata* Engelm)." *Arctic and Alpine Research* 24, no. 3 (1992): 253–56.

Cohen, Michael P. *A Garden of Bristlecones: Tales of Change in the Great Basin.* Reno: University of Nevada Press, 1998.

Connor, Kristina F., and Ronald M. Lanner. "The Architectural Significance of Interfoliar Branches in Pinus Subsection *Balfourianae.*" *Canadian Journal of Forest Research* 17 (1987): 269–72.

———. "Cuticle Thickness and Chlorophyll Content in Bristlecone Pine Needles of Various Ages." *Bulletin of the Torrey Botanical Club* 118 (1991): 184–87.

———. "Effects of Tree Age on Pollen, Seed, and Seedling Characteristics in Great Basin Bristlecone Pine." *Botanical Gazette* 152 (1991): 107–13.

———. "Effects of Tree Age on Secondary Xylem and Phloem Anatomy in Stems of Great Basin Bristlecone Pine (Pinus longaeva)." *American Journal of Botany* 77 (1990): 1070–77.

Critchfield, William B. "Hybridization of Foxtail and Bristlecone Pines." *Madroño* 24 (1977): 193–212.

Currey, Donald R. "An Ancient Bristlecone Pine Stand in Eastern Nevada." *Ecology* 46 (1965): 564–66.

Domec, J.-C., J. M. Warren, F. C. Meinzer, J. R. Brooks, and R. Coulombe. "Native Root Xylem Embolism and Stomatal Closure in Stands of Douglas-fir and Ponderosa Pine: Mitigation by Hydraulic Redistribution." *Oecologia* 141 (2004): 7–16.

Eklund, Leif, Harald Sall, and Sune Linder. "Enhanced Growth and Ethylene Increases Spiral Grain Formation in *Picea abies* and *Abies balsamea* Trees." *Trees—Structure and Function* 17 (2003): 81–86.

Ennos, Roland. *Trees.* Washington, D.C.: Smithsonian Institution Press, 2001.

Ewers, Frank W. "The Determinate and Indeterminate Dwarf Shoots of *Pinus longaeva* (Bristlecone Pine)." *Canadian Journal of Botany* 61 (1983): 2280–90.

———. "Secondary Growth in Needle Leaves of *Pinus longaeva* (Bristlecone Pine) and Other Conifers: Quantitative Data." *American Journal of Botany* 69 (1982): 1552–59.

Ewers, Frank W., and Rudolf Schmid. "Longevity of Needle Fascicles of *Pinus longaeva* (Bristlecone Pine) and Other North American Pines." *Oecologia* 51 (1981): 107–15.

Ferguson, C. W. "Bristlecone Pine: Science and Esthetics." *Science* 159 (1968): 839–46.

Finch, Caleb E. 1999. "Longevity Without Aging: Possible Examples." In J.-M. Robine, et al. (eds.), *The Paradoxes of Longevity*, Research and Perspectives in Longevity. Berlin: Springer-Verlag, 1999.

Flanary, Barry E., and Gunther Kletetschka. "Analysis of Telomere Length and Telomerase Activity in Tree Species of Various Lifespans, and with Age in the Bristlecone Pine *Pinus longaeva*." *Biogerontology* 6 (2005): 101–11.

Fritts, Harold C. "Bristlecone Pine in the White Mountains of California: Growth and Ring-Width Characteristics." Laboratory of Tree-Ring Research paper no. 4. Tucson: University of Arizona Press, 1969.

———. *Tree Rings and Climate.* London: Academic Press, 1976.

Gish, Duane T. "More Creationist Research. Part II: Biological Research." *Creation Research Society Quarterly* 26, no. 1 (June 5, 1989). http://www.creationresearch.org/crsq/articles/26/26_1a.html.

Grant, Michael C. "The Trembling Giant." *Discover*, October 1993.

Graumlich, Lisa J. "Subalpine Tree Growth, Climate, and Increasing CO_2: An Assessment of Recent Growth Trends." *Ecology* 72 (1991): 1–11.

Hall, Clarence A., Jr., ed. *Natural History of the White-Inyo Range, Eastern California*. California Natural History Guide no. 55. Berkeley: University of California Press, 1991.

Hiebert, Ronald D., and James L. Hamrick. "An Ecological Study of Bristlecone Pine (*Pinus longaeva*) in Utah and Eastern Nevada." *Great Basin Naturalist* 44 (1984): 487–94.

———. "Patterns and Levels of Genetic Variation in Great Basin Bristlecone Pine, *Pinus longaeva*." *Evolution* 37 (1983): 302–10.

Jacoby, Gordon C., and Rosanne D. D'Arrigo. "Tree Rings, Carbon Dioxide, and Climatic Change." *Proceedings of the National Academy of Sciences USA* 94 (1997): 8350–53.

Jepson, Willis Linn. *The Trees of California*. 2nd ed. Berkeley, Calif.: Sather Gate Bookshop, 1923.

Johnson, LeRoy C., and William B. Critchfield. "A White-Pollen Variant of Bristlecone Pine." *Journal of Heredity* 65 (1974): 123.

Johnson, LeRoy C., and Jean Johnson. "Methuselah: Fertile Senior Citizen." *American Forests* 84 (1978): 29–31, 43.

Koch, George W., Stephen C. Sillett, Gregory M. Jennings, and Stephen D. Davis. "The Limits to Tree Height." *Nature* 428 (2004): 851–54.

LaMarche, Valmore C., Jr. "Environment in Relation to Age of Bristlecone Pines." *Ecology* 50 (1969): 53–59.

———. "Holocene Climatic Variations Inferred from Treeline Fluctuations in the White Mountains, California." *Quaternary Research* 3 (1973): 632–60.

———. *Origin and Geologic Significance of Buttress Roots of Bristlecone Pines, White Mountains, California*. U.S. Department of the Interior, Geological Survey article 98, professional paper 475-C, 1963.

———. *Rates of Slope Degradation as Determined from Botanical Evidence, White Mountains, California*. U.S. Department of the Interior, Geological Survey professional paper 352-I, 1968.

LaMarche, Valmore C., Jr., and Harold A. Mooney. "Recent Climatic Change and Development of the Bristlecone Pine (*P. longaeva* Bailey) Krummholz Zone, Mt. Washington, Nevada." *Arctic and Alpine Research* 4 (1972): 61–72.

Lambert, Darwin. "Martyr for a Species." *Audubon* 70 (1968): 50–55.

Lanner, Ronald M. *Conifers of California*. Los Olivos, Calif.: Cachuma Press, 1999.

———. "Dependence of Great Basin Bristlecone Pine on Clark's Nutcracker for Regeneration at High Elevations." *Arctic and Alpine Research* 20 (1988): 358–62.

———. *Made for Each Other: A Symbiosis of Birds and Pines*. New York: Oxford University Press, 1996.

———. *Trees of the Great Basin*. Reno: University of Nevada Press, 1984.

———. "Whatever Became of the World's Oldest Tree?" *Wildflower* 12 (1996): 26–27.

———. "Why Do Trees Live So Long?" *Ageing Research Reviews* 1 (2002): 653–71.

Lanner, Ronald M., and Kistina F. Connor. "Does Bristlecone Pine Senesce?" *Experimental Gerontology* 36 (2001): 675–85.

Larson, Douglas W. "The Paradox of Great Longevity in a Short-Lived Tree Species." *Experimental Gerontology* 36 (2001): 651–73.

Larson, Douglas W., J. Doubt, and U. Matthes-Sears. "Radially Sectored Hydraulic Pathways in the Xylem of *Thuja occidentalis* as Revealed by the Use of Dyes." *International Journal of Plant Sciences* 155 (1994): 569–82.

Lee, Seok-Woo, F. Thomas Ledig, and David R. Johnson. "Genetic Variation at Allozyme and RAPD Markers in *Pinus longaeva* (Pinaceae) of the White Mountains, California." *American Journal of Botany* 89 (2002): 566–77.

Lloyd, Andrea H. "Response of Tree-line Populations of Foxtail Pine (*Pinus balfouriana*) to Climate Variation over the Last 1000 Years." *Canadian Journal of Forest Research* 27 (1997): 936–42.

Lorey, Frank. "Tree Rings and Biblical Chronology." Institute for Creation Research (1994). http://www.icr.org/article/381.

Mastrogiuseppe, R. J., and J. D. Mastrogiuseppe. "A Study of *Pinus balfouriana* Grev. & Balf. (Pinaceae)." *Systematic Botany* 5 (1980): 86–104.

Mattheck, C. *Trees: The Mechanical Design*. Berlin: Springer Verlag, 1991.

McDonald, G. I., B. A. Richardson, P. J. Zambino, N. B. Klopfenstein, and M.-S. Kim. "*Pedicularis* and *Castilleja* Are Natural Hosts of *Cronartium ribicola* in North America: A First Report." *Forest Pathology* 36 (2006): 73–82.

Millar, C. I. "Impact of the Eocene on the Evolution of *Pinus* L." *Annals of the Missouri Botanical Garden* 80 (1993): 471–98.

Muench, David, and Darwin Lambert. *Timberline Ancients*. Portland, Oreg.: Charles H. Belding, 1972.

Muir, John. *The Mountains of California*. Garden City, N.Y.: Doubleday, 1894 (1961).

Oline, David K., Jeffry B. Mitton, and Michael C. Grant. "Population and Subspecific Genetic Differentiation in the Foxtail Pine (*Pinus balfouriana*)." *Evolution* 54 (2000): 1813–19.

Orians, Colin M., Margaret M. I. Van Vuuren, Nancy L. Harris, Benjamin A. Babst, and George S. Ellmore. "Differential Sectoriality in Long-Distance Transport in Temperate Tree Species: Evidence from Dye Flow, 15N Transport, and Vessel Element Pitting." *Trees—Structure and Function* 18 (2004): 501–9.

Panshin, A. J., and Carl de Zeeuw. *Textbook of Wood Technology*. 3rd ed. Vol. 1. New York: McGraw-Hill, 1970.

Peterson, David L., Michael J. Arbaugh, Lindsay J. Robinson, and Berg R. Derderian. "Growth Trends of Whitebark Pine and Lodgepole Pine in a Subalpine Sierra Nevada Forest, California, U.S.A." *Arctic and Alpine Research* 22 (1990): 233–43.

Reich, Peter B., Jacek Oleksyn, Jerzy Modrzynski, and Mark G. Tjoelker. "Evidence That Longer Needle Retention of Spruce and Pine Populations at High Elevations and High Latitudes Is Largely a Phenotypic Response." *Tree Physiology* 16 (1996): 643–47.

Rourke, Michael D. "Foxtail pine—*Pinus balfouriana*." http://www.palomar.edu/
mnhsdivision/Foxtails.

———. "A Preliminary Cladistic Analysis of the Balfourianae Pines Based Strictly
on Published Character Data." In *Natural History of the White-Inyo Range, Eastern
California and Western Nevada and High Altitude Physiology*. Vol. 1. University of
California White Mountain Research Station Symposium, 1986, 77–83.

Schauer, Andrew J., Anna W. Schoettle, and Richard L. Boyce. "Partial Cambial
Mortality in High-Elevation *Pinus aristata* (Pinaceae)." *American Journal of
Botany* 88 (2001): 646–52.

Schubert, Gilbert H., and W. J. Rietveld. *Bristlecone Pine—Its Phenology, Cone
Maturity, and Seed Production in the San Francisco Peaks, Arizona*. U.S. Department
of Agriculture, Forest Service research note RM-180, 1970.

Schulman, Edmund. "Bristlecone Pine, Oldest Known Living Thing." *National
Geographic* 113 (1958): 354–72.

———. *Dendroclimatic Changes in Semiarid America*. Tucson: University of Arizona
Press, 1956.

———. "Longevity Under Adversity in Conifers. *Science* 119 (1954): 396–99.

———. "Over-age Drought Conifers of the Rocky Mountains." *Journal of Forestry*
41 (1943): 422–27.

Skatter, Sondre, and Bohumil Kucera. "The Cause of the Prevalent Directions of
the Spiral Grain Patterns in Conifers." *Trees—Structure and Function* 12 (1998):
265–73.

Sudworth, George B. *The Pine Trees of the Rocky Mountain Region*. U.S. Department
of Agriculture, bulletin 460. Washington, D.C.: Government Printing Office,
1917.

Tasmania Department of Primary Industries and Water. "Kings Lomatia: The
Oldest Plant Clone in the World?" http://www.dpiw.tas.gov.au/inter.nsf/
WebPages/BHAN-54A7XU?open.

Thomas, Howard. "Ageing in Plants." *Mechanisms of Ageing and Development* 123
(2002): 747–53.

Thompson, R. S., and J. I. Mead. "Late Quaternary Environments and Bio-
geography in the Great Basin." *Quaternary Research* 17 (1982): 39–55.

Vaillancourt, Rene. "The Oldest Living Plant Individual." *Botanical Electronic
News* 149 (November 8, 1996). http://www.ou.edu/cas/botany-micro/ben/
1996.shtml.

Van Gelderen, D. M., and J. R. P. Van Hoey Smith. *Conifers: The Illustrated Encyc-
lopedia*. Vol. 2. Portland, Oreg.: Timber Press, 1996.

Vasek, Frank C. "Creosote Bush: Long-lived Clones in the Mojave Desert."
American Journal of Botany 67 (1980): 246–55.

Wagener, Willis W. "Longevity Under Adversity in Conifers" (letter). *Science* 119
(1954): 883–84.

Wright, R. D., and Harold A. Mooney. "Substrate-Oriented Distribution of
Bristlecone Pine in the White Mountains of California." *American Midland
Naturalist* 73 (1965): 257–84.

Zimmermann, Martin H., and Claud L. Brown. *Trees: Structure and Function*. New
York: Springer Verlag, 1971.

Glossary

amino acid: Components of proteins that contain the NH_2 amino group.

annual ring: In temperate-zone trees, the growth of earlywood and latewood of a year seen in cross section.

anthocyanin: A pigment producing blue to red coloration in plants.

bark: The dead and living tissues outside a tree's cambium layer.

bark strip: A vertical strip of living tissue on a tree trunk, with deadwood on either side.

bud: The embryonic components of a shoot, under a protective cover of scales.

buttress root: In very old bristlecone pines, roots that have been exposed by soil erosion, and thus are growing only on the lower surface.

cambium: The film of tissue just outside the most recent annual sheath of wood, the cells of which divide to produce the xylem (wood) and phloem (inner bark) cells forming woody stems. Syn. vascular cambium.

carbohydrate: A compound of carbon, hydrogen, and oxygen, forming sugars, starches, and cellulose, which in green plants is made by photosynthesis.

chlorophyll: The green photosynthetic pigment found in the cells of higher plants.

clone: A group of plants that have arisen by vegetative means from the same individual, and are thus genetically identical.

compression wood: Dense wood that is formed on the lower surfaces of conifer branches and trunks and exerts an upward pressure.

cone: The pollen-bearing or seed-bearing reproductive structure of a conifer. See also **pollen cone** and **seed cone**.

conelet: In pines, the unpollinated new seed cone emerging from its bud.

cork cambium: The tissue of dividing cells within the bark that gives rise to new bark cells.

cortex: In a young woody shoot or root, the tissue just inside the outer skin, or epidermis.

cotyledon: A tuft of delicate needle leaves that form in the embryo and become the first leaves of the seedling.

Cretaceous: The last period of the Mesozoic era, during which dinosaurs became extinct, the Rocky Mountains formed, and flowering plants appeared.

cuticle: The waxy outer covering of a leaf, which prevents excessive water loss.

damping-off: A disease of seedlings caused by fungi, especially *Fusarium* and *Phytophthore.*

dendrochronology: The science of using tree rings to study past climates and other phenomena.

dormancy: In pines, a resting condition terminated by a required chilling period followed by a warming period.

earlywood: The portion of an annual ring formed early in the growth season. Syn. springwood.

enzyme: A complex protein that acts as a catalyst for biochemical reactions in an organism.

epicormic branch: A branch that arises on the trunk or limb of a tree from a bud that lies dormant beneath the bark.

epidermis: A thin layer of cells that forms an outer skin for a plant part.

fascicle: A group of pine needles, the number depending on the species, fastened at the base.

fascicle sheath: The papery tissue that surrounds the base of the needle fascicle, and which in the foxtail and bristlecone pines usually falls off by the fascicle's second year.

fatty acid: A component of fats and oils.

fertilization: The act of fusion of a sperm and an egg in which the full chromosome number of the species is restored and the initiation of an individual is begun.

foxtail: In pines of the subsection *Balfourianae*, the long, heavily needled end of a branch, also called a tassel. When capitalized, the common name for pines of the subsection *Balfourianae*.

foxtail pine: The common name of the species *Pinus balfouriana*, one of three species of pines of the subsection *Balfourianae*.

genotype: The genetic constitution of an individual.

germination: The development of a seed into a seedling.

growing season: The portion of the year from last spring frost to first fall frost.

heartwood: The wood deep within a stem in which water is no longer transported due to clogged cells.

hormone: A substance formed in one part of a plant, usually the foliage or roots, that is transported to another part where it has a specific effect.

hybridization: The interbreeding of different species.

inner bark: See phloem.

interfoliar bud: In pines, a bud that forms within a needle fascicle.

interglacial: The time between glacial periods.

isozyme: One of several forms of the same enzyme.

juvenile needles: In pines, the single (nonfascicled) needles produced in seedlings, sometimes for several years.

krummholz: Stunted growth form induced by severe growth conditions, usually in conifers at treeline.

latewood: The portion of the annual ring formed late in the growth season. Syn. summerwood.

leader: The leading shoot of a tree. Syn. terminal.

lignin: A polymer that, with cellulose, forms the walls of xylem (wood) cells.

longevity: The length of an organism's life.

Mesozoic: The era that includes the Triassic, Jurassic, and Cretaceous periods; also called the Age of Reptiles.

mutation: A spontaneous change in an organism's genetic material.

mycorrhiza: A symbiosis between a fungus and the roots of a plant.

needle: The long, narrow leaf of a conifer.

oleoresin: In conifers, the sticky, aromatic fluid, composed largely of terpenes, that oozes from injured tissues such as stems, roots, and cones. Syns. resin, pitch.

ovule: The oval body borne on the inside of a conifer conelet scale, which contains an egg cell and develops into a seed following fertilization.

phenotype: The characteristics of an organism determined by the interaction of the environment on its genetic constitution, or genotype.

phloem: The conductive tissue between the bark and the cambium that carries dissolved sugars and other substances from the crown to other areas of a tree. Syn. inner bark.

photosynthesis: The biological process in green plants that uses light energy to produce sugars from water and carbon dioxide.

pit: An opening in the wall of a cell giving access to a neighboring cell.

pitch: See oleoresin.

pith: A thin rod of tissue running down the center of the shoot and around which the first annual ring forms.

Pleistocene: The first epoch of the Quaternary period, typified by repeated episodes of glaciation.

pollen cone: In pines, a small, nonwoody, cylindrical reproductive structure made up of pollen-bearing sacs spirally arranged on an axis, and found in clusters just below the new needles at the end of a growing shoot.

pollen grain: In conifers, a golden, several-celled, wind-dispersed structure formed in male cones, containing a sperm cell that fertilizes the egg cell in the ovule.

pollination: In conifers, the arrival of wind-borne pollen grains into the open mouths of the ovules.

ray: In pine wood, one of many radially oriented strands of tissue crossing the annual rings, appearing like spokes of a wheel in a cross section.

resin: See oloeoresin.

resin canal: In pines, an opening between cells, especially in the wood where canals may extend many meters in the trunk, lined with cells that secrete resin. Syn. resin duct.

root graft: The anatomical connection of roots of two or more trees, allowing the transfer from tree to tree of water, nutrients, hormones, and fungal spores.

sap: A solution that circulates through a tree's vascular system. Xylem sap is the solution of mineral nutrients taken up from the soil through the roots and carried through the trunk and branches. Phloem sap is the solution of sugars formed through photosynthesis in the needles (in pines) and carried through the inner bark.

sapling: A young tree.

sapwood: The outer, most recently formed annual rings, through which water and nutrients taken up from the soil are transported.

sector: In some trees, a major root and the trunk and branches to which it supplies water, to the exclusion of other sectors.

seed cone: In conifers, the semiwoody reproductive structure composed of seed-bearing scales arranged spirally on a stalk, usually requiring three separate growth years to produce mature seed.

seedling: A recently germinated seed, or the resulting tree while still small and young.

senescence: The irreversible changes brought about by age that lead to death.

shoot: In conifers, a stem bearing needles.

shoot apex: A dome-shaped mass of cells that is protected within a bud, and whose growth gives rise to the next year's bud when the current bud grows into a shoot.

sieve cell: A cell in the phloem that is aligned with other similar cells to form a tube, within which dissolved sugars and hormones flow up or down the tree.

spiral grain: An orientation of wood cells left or right of vertical, visible if bark is removed.

stomate: Microscopic openings, on leaf and other epidermal surfaces, that control water loss.

stratify: To store seeds in moist sand under refrigeration to increase germination rate.

taproot: A root that grows vertically.

telomere: A specialized structure at the end of a chromosome consisting of repeated DNA sequences.

tracheid: The basic cell of coniferous wood, the function of which is to transport water and strengthen stems.

vascular bundle: In conifer needles, the vein of the needle, consisting of xylem and phloem.

vascular cambium: See **cambium.**

water stress: Physiological stress due to insufficient water.

white pine blister rust: A serious disease of five-needled pines, imported form Europe in the early 1900s, which has spread to most North American white pines.

wing: In conifers, the membrane-like extensions of seeds, formed from cone scale tissue, which allow the seeds to be carried by the wind.

xylem: The plant tissue that transports water and strengthens the stem. Syn. wood.

Index

trunks, 68–69; and shoot, 20
Buprestids, 74

Callahan, Frank, 14, 58
cambium, 32, 34–35, 66: and annual
ring, 36; and bark strips, 64; and
longevity, 57; protection of, 40; of
roots, 32
cambium, cork, 40
carbohydrates, 24, 27, 33, 44, 81
carbon dioxide, 24, 78
"cat faces," 94
'Cecilia' (cultivar), 63
Cedar Breaks National Monument (UT), 8
Cerambycids, 74
Charleston (Spring) Mountains (NV), 7
chlorophyll, 23, 26
chromosomes, 59
Clark's Nutcracker, 29–31, 71, 72, 74, 96
Clear Lake (CA), 16
climate change, 18, 76–79, 81
clones, box huckleberry, 99; creosote
bush, 98; differences from freestanding trees, 101–102; King's holly,
99, 101; quaking aspen, 99, 100. See also
treelets
coast redwood (Sequoia sempervirens), 37,
51, 68, 84
Cochetopa Pass (CO), 12
color: of cones, 30; of sapwood, 74
Colorado pinyon pine (Pinus edulis), 84, 92
common juniper (Juniperus communis), 94
compression wood, 51, 66
cones. See seed cones; pollen cones
Connor, Kristina, 34, 55, 64, 90–91
core analysis, 84, 86–87, 88, 90
cork cambium, 40
Cox, Don, 88
creationists, 17
creosote bush (Larrea tridentata), 98
Critchfield, William (Bill) B., 47
crown asymmetry, 74–75
cultivars, 63
currant, 81

Currey, Donald R., 87–88
cuticle, 24, 26

decay, 44, 48, 54, 74, 90, 94
Deep Creek Range (UT), 7
dimensions, 58
disease, 76, 79, 81–82
distribution, geographic, 3, 16
Dixie National Forest (UT), 80, 92, 93, 97
DNA, 57
dolomite, 45, 47
Douglas fir (Pseudotsuga menziesii), 84
'Dwarf Form' (cultivar), 63

earlywood, 35–36, 37
elephant's head (Pedicularis), 83
elliptical crowns, 74–75
Engelmann, George, 8
Engelmann spruce (Picea engelmannii), 17, 89
Ennos, Roland, 38
epicormic branches, 20, 23, 41, 54, 91
epidermis, 24, 40
erosion, 31, 32, 54, 64, 65, 66, 72, 94, 97
etiquette, trail, 9
eucalyptus, 48

fascicles, needle, 10, 20, 21, 22, 23, 24,
48, 91
Fairplay (CO), 12
false rings, 17
Finch, C. E. ("Tuck"), 96
fire, forest, 2, 40, 54, 76, 79, 80, 81, 94
fire scars, 94
Fish Creek Range (NV), 7
Flanary, Barry, 59
'Formal Form' (cultivar), 63
forms and shapes, 61–75
fossils, 16
foxtail pine (Pinus balfouriana), 12–16, 41;
cones, 30; cultivars of, 63; dimensions,
58; disease in, 82; identification,
13–14; krummholz form, 53–54;
location of, 3, 14, 16; mature, 52;
nomenclature and subspecies,

ABOUT THE AUTHOR

Born in Brooklyn, New York, **Ronald M. Lanner** was trained as a forester at New York State's College of Environmental Science and Forestry and later earned a Ph.D. in forest botany and genetics at the University of Minnesota. He was a research forester with the U.S. Forest Service in California and Hawaii, and he taught courses in tree biology at Utah State University for many years. Lanner is currently emeritus visiting scientist at the Institute of Forest Genetics in Placerville, California. He is the author of numerous papers and five books about trees, including *Made for Each Other: A Symbiosis of Birds and Pines* and *Conifers of California*. In his books, Lanner strives to interpret scientific findings for the general reader in a simple and accurate manner, and to present fresh information not readily available to the public. His research has taken him all over the world, but he has always returned to the mountains of the American West and the haunts of the bristlecone and foxtail pines.